Yankee on the Prairie

Howard R. Barnard of Kansas — Pioneer Educator

For Newton,
Ray Newton,
May you keep on
pioneering for old Fort.
Hays State! Warmest
Regards
Allen R. Miller
4/97

Yankee on the Prairie

Howard R. Barnard of Kansas — Pioneer Educator

by Allan R. Miller

With Foreword by Joanna L. Stratton,
author of *Pioneer Women*

Sunflower University Press

1531 Yuma (Box 1009), Manhattan, Kansas 66502-4228 USA

ISBN 0-89745-184-8

Cover: by Michael Florian Jilg

Edited by Sandra J. Rose

Layout by Lori L. Daniel

For Sandi and Corey

Contents

Foreword

$\mathcal{E}$VERY now and then, a figure emerges from the obscurity of our past to remind us that America, more than any other nation, has been built by ordinary people leading extraordinary lives. Allan Miller's splendid volume on the life of Howard Barnard does just that. At its heart, *Yankee on the Prairie* is the story of a pioneer educator who was every bit the American hero. With painstaking detail, Allan Miller has reconstructed the life history of Howard Barnard, a most unique individual who led an unconventional life for his times but who made enormous contributions to his community and his profession. As Miller relates, Barnard was a man undeterred by hardship and unswayed by public opinion. Firm in his beliefs and determined in his goals, he excelled at what he loved best — teaching school and building libraries — and in the process, he achieved a measure of lasting greatness.

In the main, Howard Barnard exemplified the very best aspects of those who pioneered the American West. Caught by the national fervor for pioneering, Barnard, like so many others of his time, heeded those immortal words of Horace Greeley: "*Go West, young man.*" Leaving behind the comforts of a privileged life in the East, he set his sights on Kansas and headed West to make his mark. But while other adventurers filled their covered wagons with farming tools and housewares, Howard Barnard brought with him little more than a love of books and an appreciation of children. With ingenuity and fortitude, he faced life's struggles with a measure of rugged perseverance and hardy individualism. Although he himself was not a homesteader, he struggled alongside those early settlers to transform Kansas from a frontier wilderness into a flourishing society. Others sought to tame the land by building homesteads and starting towns, but Howard Barnard conspired to tame its people with reading, writing, and arithmetic.

In the earliest years of the Kansas frontier, the prairie wilderness offered the young few avenues for traditional learning, and the prospects for organized schooling were exceedingly dim. Settlers struggling to eke out an existence from an inhospitable environment lacked the financial wherewithal to build real schools. Yet most parents, though not themselves well educated, recognized that education was vital to the advancement of their families and the betterment of their communities. With few resources at hand, pioneer ingenuity ruled, and it was not uncommon to find the early homesteaders creating makeshift schools in their soddies and dugouts. If the pioneer mother was literate, it was invariably she who took on the responsibilities of teaching the young in the cabin classroom where the hard dirt floor substituted as a blackboard and the family Bible served as a text. It was a haphazard process that led one pioneer woman to exclaim, "The miracle was that a love of learning ever survived the rigors of the school days then. But it did."

For those early pioneers intent on having some measure of schooling, however primitive, the arrival of a dedicated educator like Howard Barnard must have seemed a godsend. Here was a man born into a family of renowned scholars and imbued from childhood with an understanding of educational theory. Possessing real books of his own and determined to teach at all costs, Howard Barnard was a rare schoolmaster indeed, and luckily for the children of Rush County, Kansas, he was anxious to challenge the practices of the day with educational theories of his own. Sparing no expense and dedicating his entire inheritance to his pupils, he let nothing stand in his way.

Yet Barnard's efforts to educate people went far beyond the classroom itself. With an intense love of books and a passion for the etiquette of reading, he was determined to bestow on the people of LaCrosse his most precious possession of all: *his library*. To a farm community of modest means, his collection of some 3,000 volumes must have been a remarkable largess.

Howard Barnard's contribution was enormous, and he left his mark on many generations of early Kansans. It is not surprising that he was a walking legend around Rush County, Kansas. What is surprising is that his contributions to the settlement of the state have been so largely forgotten. Allan Miller is to be applauded for resurrecting the life story of Howard Barnard and for reminding us that our nation has been built on the backs of men and women with such vision, ingenuity, and fortitude. Howard Barnard is one of those unsung heroes whose name has long since been forgotten but whose legacy lives on in our collective heritage. He was a true pioneer in the finest sense of the word.

Joanna L. Stratton
Author of *Pioneer Women*

Howard Barnard, fall 1944. This photo by Larry's Photography of LaCrosse, won first prize at the Kansas State Fair. (Photo, Barnard Library, LaCrosse, KS)

Preface

A concern of historians has been the neglected story of the common man: sometimes thought to be unimportant; sometimes lost because there are few, if any, records or relics to document it.

This biography of Howard Barnard is the life story of one of those common men who, like so many others, made a remarkable contribution to America's saga. Through his life, one can see the challenges facing those hearty Americans who tried and succeeded in taming the American frontier during the latter part of the 19th century. One can also gain insight into the challenges facing American education and its powerful potential to acculturate America's young people who lived on the "edge of civilization."

Howard Barnard, born in New York City in 1863, was the great-nephew of Henry Barnard, who, along with Horace Mann, was one of America's most influential and prominent educators in the mid-19th century. Howard's great-uncle Henry was the first United States Commissioner of Education, appointed by President Andrew Johnson; was the president of the University of Wisconsin; and founded the *American Journal of Education*, the first of its kind in the United States.

Howard Barnard, fortuitously for America and Kansas, chose his uncle as his hero. Howard devoted his life to teaching children, building libraries, and bringing culture to the American frontier by demonstrating a reverence for books. He attempted to put his great-uncle's theories of education into practice to see if they would work on the plains of the American West.

At one point in his life, Howard Barnard sank his family fortune into the founding of an innovative experimental school he called Entre Nous, near McCracken, Kansas. Near the end of his life, he stated that the founding of the school, although short-lived, was his crowning achievement. In 1906, the school was among the first in the United States to implement busing of students, as the responsibility of the school. Entre Nous School was also one of the first in the country to be formed by consolidating several rural schools.

And Barnard pioneered the idea that physical education and athletic programs should be as equally accessible for girls as for boys. Ironically, even in his later life, Barnard had no idea that he was an innovator of these important educational concepts. Like so many common Americans before and since, he merely thought he was doing his job as a teacher in the best manner he knew for his "little scholars."

After the closing of the Entre Nous educational experiment, Barnard devoted the remainder of his long life to his love of books. At LaCrosse, Kansas, as the town's first librarian, he owned all of the books, which gave an interesting twist to Benjamin Franklin's idea of a free, publicly supported lending library. Yet Barnard loaned any book he had to anyone who wanted to read it. He also hauled his books around in a wagon from one community to another, bringing culture to the plains of western Kansas. At one point, it took four horse-drawn farm wagons to haul his more than 3,000 volumes. He was not the typical librarian — he was more like a medicine-show salesman advocating books as a general panacea for the cultural ills of the frontier.

Andy Warhohl, pop artist and experimental filmmaker, stated that every person who does anything remarkable receives 15 minutes of fame. In 1946, Barnard finally received his fleeting renown when he was 83 years old. *Reader's Digest* carried his story, as recorded by writer Ralph Wallace. Subsequently, Barnard received hundreds of fan letters and an offer to make his life story into a Hollywood movie — a preposterous idea to Barnard.

Barnard's memorial, and a most fitting one, is the LaCrosse, Kansas, library, The Barnard Library, named in his honor. Barnard gave his books to the cause and served as its first librarian, enjoying ten years in this elegant and useful little building made of native Kansas limestone, before dying at the age of 85 in 1948. It is unfortunate that thousands of Americans — and Kansans — have never heard of him, his intellectual courage, and his momentous contributions to America, its frontier, and its educational history. This biography tries to remedy the oversight.

My personal interest in Barnard's life began in 1972 when I became the newest member of the Fort Hays State University School of Education. The university is just 20 miles from where Barnard founded Entre Nous School near McCracken. Dr. Bill Robinson, an educational historian, chided me that I had never heard of "the famous Barnard of Kansas." I thought he was talking about Commissioner Henry Barnard and had added the "from Kansas" as a bit of color commentary. When students periodically presented reports about Howard Barnard of LaCrosse, Kansas, as part of an assignment on Kansas educators, I became intrigued. Some of their stories, gathered from old-timers who knew Barnard, were incredible.

Finally, some 15 years later, I began researching Howard Barnard. Some of the local legends could be verified; others could not. Yet, his life story was captivating, nonetheless.

Of course, there are no pioneers of his stature left. Consequently, it is my hope that others will dig deeply into their own local history to try to find the uncommon amongst the commonplace. If that happens occasionally, then it will have been well worth the hours spent uncovering the incredible life of Howard Barnard, Yankee on the Prairie.

Acknowledgments

I owe this labor of love to many people. My wife, Sandi, not only encouraged me when life at the university was bearing down and taking time away from the writing, but read chapters and offered editorial and content suggestions. My teenage son, Corey, gave me incentive by comparing my writing to his own papers written for high school assignments. Without their support, the book would not have been written.

Three graduate students in my History of American Education class first brought Barnard to my attention with excellent research papers on a "local educator": Rex Gebhard, David Legleiter, and Becky Stephenson. They whetted my appetite.

Three prominent citizens from Rush County, Kansas, came to my rescue at every turn when I was lost or puzzled by some local historical occasion or person. Elva Paustian, the librarian at Barnard Library in LaCrosse, carries on the tradition of Howard Barnard in a friendly, efficient, and even courageous manner. Every time I entered her library, she had found some new piece of the Barnard puzzle and was anxious to share her discovery. Carolyn Thompson and Shirley Higgins, the historians-in-residence at McCracken's modern country library, took time from their ranching and families to spend many hours helping and taking me to various locations around McCracken to get the "lay of the land" and to put it in the historical context of when Barnard was working in the area 100 years earlier. I am indebted to their enthusiasm for this biography, as well as their own excellent research in the history of their small town.

At Fort Hays State University, several people sustained me by offering advice about the manuscript, library research, and the writing of history: Jim Forsythe, my graduate dean and historian in his own right; Ray Wilson, of our history department and the most published faculty member at FHSU; Mac Reed, a government documents librarian supreme; Esta Lou Riley, our Western Special Collections librarian; Mike Kallan, whose knowledge of geneaology was critical; Judy Pape, whom I bothered constantly for library media and computer help; Jim Vequest, who worked on a computerized map of Rush County; Mick Jilg, who enthusiastically took up the call to put his prize-winning artistic talent to work on the cover even though he was recuperating from an accident and could hardly move a muscle; Bob Chalender, my department chair; Tom Pickering, my dean; Jim Murphy, my provost, who supported my research effort by promoting my sabbatical leave; and Maurice Witten, who may be the only man alive who understood the x-ray machine that Barnard used as a teaching tool.

Several graduate assistants became so interested in Barnard that they wanted to help in any way possible to bring him to life through this book: Kathleen Keener, Dave Otis, Bruce Coulson, Sherry Giebler, Melissa Bean, and Kathy Schmidtberger. These dedicated people helped by reading newspapers on microfilm, raising the task to an art form that was fun and a type of celebration. All are now professional educators teaching and counseling in Kansas.

I was excited to find Darlienne Thompson Werhahn living on a beautiful farm near Larned, for it was her article written over 50 years ago that became my North Star for the life of Barnard. I spent one of the best afternoons of my life with her, her husband, and her sister, Virginia Taylor, talking about old times in Kansas and, in particular, about Howard Barnard.

Eileen McChristian arranged for me to interview her mother, Rosa Schnert, in the LaCrosse Nursing Home. It was Rosa, Dudley Shutte, and the late Ruby Thompson who provided the colorful commentary for the book because they had worked so closely with Barnard and remembered him so well. I recall sitting at Ruby's kitchen table with Carolyn Thompson in McCracken, trying to keep Ruby talking about Entre Nous when she really wanted to talk about the LaCrosse-McCracken wars. Ruby was in her mid-90s, living very well alone, thank you! A tough and thoughtful Kansan!

I discovered that the Rush County Courthouse has some of the nicest public servants working anywhere today. The help I received from Register of Deeds Mary Ann Pechanec, and her assistant, Gloria Anders, was truly professional. And Virginia Keener, the Deputy Clerk of the District Court, aided in the search for important documents in her office.

Churches are also great sources for historians. Betty MacDonald was most helpful with some of the Barnard geneaology in the Hays Church of Jesus Christ of Latter-day Saints. I am also indebted to the minister of the First Baptist Church in Hays, Jerry Sprock, and parishioner and neighbor Rita Hauck, for providing a Baptist hymnal that included the hymn "Higher Ground."

My trips to Topeka to research Barnard at the Kansas Historical Research Center were always pleasant because of the people working there. I especially appreciated Leslie Cade, Terry Harmon, Jane Kelsey, Marian Bond, and doing yet another project with, in my opinion, the best photo document historian in the United States, Nancy Sherbert. Another librarian-historian who was most helpful was Mary Ann Thompson, who directs the Kansas Room of the Hays Public Library.

I wish to thank Bill and Fran Barnard of Seattle, Washington; Judith Schiff of Yale University, New Haven, Connecticut; and Karen Hartford of Trinity College, Hartford, Connecticut.

As good fortune would have it, I had an excellent publisher in Carol

Williams and came rapidly to appreciate what a good copy editor like
Sandra Rose could do for a manuscript.

Fate allowed me to meet Joanna Stratton when we were at Stanford
University at the same time in 1981. Our shared interest in Kansas keeps
us in touch. Her Foreword is very special to me and to this book. And,
finally, at a very critical point in the development of the book, a former
student of Howard Barnard's, Robert E. Schmidt of Hays, stepped forward with his very special help, keen insight, and support.

Chapter 1

Childhood in the East

Proud Kansas, known on land and sea
Happy the man on foreign strand
Who hails from thee! In any land
On earth, a Kansan let him stand,
This name shall be his passport free.
   — from Moody's "Song of Kansas"

New York! What a City!

WHAT Athens was to ancient Greece and Rome to the Roman Empire, New York had become to America by the mid-19th century. It had surpassed all other U.S. cities as the center for cultural, political, and economic power. Yet, aside from the concerns of their own city, many New Yorkers at this time were fascinated by the concerns of a territory nearly 1,500 miles west of them — "bleeding Kansas"!

While Kansans and New Yorkers have always been rather strange bedfellows, they have been unusually interested in each other's development and culture. The first sign of this was certainly the ante-bellum days of the 1850s when the Kansas-Nebraska Act was passed in May 1854. That Act divided the vast, unorganized territory west of Minnesota, Iowa, and Missouri into Kansas and Nebraska. And provisions were made for the settlers, rather than Congress, to decide whether or not to permit slavery. Many New Yorkers were finally convinced that if more pro-slavery states were to be admitted to the Union, the South would be a nuisance that would have to be dealt with.

New Yorkers by the hundreds took up the call to save Kansas from slavery. They raised money to provide "Beecher Bibles" — carbine rifles named for the outspoken Brooklyn abolitionist minister, Henry Ward Beecher — to new Kansas settlers. As every Kansas schoolboy or schoolgirl knows, Beecher Bibles were used to scare away Southern renegades from Missouri who were infiltrating the Kansas Territory in order to influence the outcome of the vote. New York City was the main monetary source for Eli Thayer's Emigrant Aid Society, which was the collection medium for the Kansas guns. Thayer was a Massachusetts schoolteacher who had founded this society to recruit people to migrate to Kansas and advocate for its admission into the Union as a free state. Originally the Massachusetts Emigrant Aid Society, it was later changed to the New England Aid Society and was commonly known as the Emigrant Aid Society. It did more than transport *people* to Kansas.

By 1856, Horace Greeley, editor of the *New York Tribune*, joined in the anti-slavery movement. Before long, the editors of other major New York newspapers took up the cause. New York Republicans, Democrats, ex-Whigs, Free-Soilers, and a "duke's variety" of other city moralists joined the movement to "Save Kansas" from pro-slavery forces. A metropolitan campaign to raise funds for "the suffering free men of Kansas" was so successful that it helped Kansas become a free rather than a slave state. The close connection between New York and Kansas was off to a rousing start.

By the decade of the 1860s, New York City's population neared one million. Thousands of its residents watched as the all-steel ship, *The Monitor*, was launched to aid the Union cause in the Civil War. However, by July 1863, thousands of the city's young men were not so sure that they wanted to fight for the Union cause. The New York City Draft Act riots occurred when President Lincoln reluctantly issued a draft order across the North. As a result, about 1,000 citizens were killed or injured, with property damage set at $1 million.

The newly arrived Irish were most opposed to the draft. They had no particular loyalty to their new government, and they resented a provision that allowed those who could afford it to buy an exemption for $300, a sum beyond their reach. The issue of race, to a certain extent, motivated the riots. The Irish thought that a war in support of blacks, whom they fiercely competed against for jobs in New York, was totally ridiculous. As a result, most of the people killed in the riots were either blacks or Irish gang members from lower Manhattan.

The riots might never have taken place had the militia, normally stationed in New York, been there to observe the draft lottery. However, the South had made its northernmost thrust, forcing the New York militia into duty at Gettysburg, the small Pennsylvania town that would later become symbolic of another sad day in American history.

On Saturday, July 11, 1863, the *New York Tribune* printed 1,200 names that were initially drawn in the draft. It announced that additional names would be pulled from a drum at the draft office at Third Avenue and 46th Street the following Monday. On that morning, the Irish resistance in the form of several thousand men pushed aside nearly 800 police, stoned the building, and burned it to the ground. Elsewhere, mobs stopped all public transportation around the city, burned and looted homes and stores, and nearly captured the mayor. By afternoon, an orphanage for black children was burned. Miraculously, authorities evacuated 233 children minutes before the disaster. Monday night, with the situation totally out of control, mobs hanged a black man in the downtown area. The next morning, another black was killed, and the destruction continued. The riots did not even subside when Governor Horatio Seymour declared a suspension of the draft. Finally, on Thursday, 10,000 National Guard troops invaded the city and restored peace and order.

Into this troublesome surrounding, Howard Robert Barnard was born on September 14, 1863, in a New York hotel. Little did he or his parents know that he was bound for Kansas Territory. Of his 85 years, he would spend only 20 in New York. They were years not wasted on war, but

High above the banks of the River Tees, in southwest County Durham, England, stand the remains of Barnard Castle, built in the Middle Ages, where the Barnard family traces its ancestral roots. (Photo, Allan Miller)

years spent accumulating all things positive that New York City and the Barnard family had to offer.

Barnard's father, Chauncey Barnard, III, was a wealthy railroad broker. Railroads were the wave of the future, and many people willingly risked their financial lives on the hope that they could pick the good railroads from the bad, with the opportunity to make a fortune. Howard Barnard's father was one of many New York financiers who made a good living obliging those willing to invest in railways. Barnard's mother, Harriet, was a second cousin to her husband. She was charming and well-educated and devoted to Howard and his younger brother and sister. Barnard often said that his mother was the inspiration of his early life in New York.

Barnard spent the school months, September through May, in New York City, living with his parents in a hotel. But each year he could hardly wait until school was out to move to the Barnard summer home in the

This is the only known photo of Howard Barnard's mother, Harriet W. Barnard. Barnard possibly carried a similar picture of his mother in his wallet. (Photo, Barnard Library, LaCrosse, KS)

country in Middletown, New York, to which the family traveled by horse and carriage. During his youth, Barnard loved staying at Middletown, and he especially relished the home's library, which was large and positioned between two main parts of the house. It had a skylight of plate glass in the ceiling, and in the center was a fountain. One project that Barnard began as a young boy was counting the books in the room. But he had never finished, because he became weary and discouraged when he had reached 6,000 volumes.

Whenever Barnard was disciplined by his parents or disagreed with his brother, he spent hours or perhaps a whole day in the library. It became his sanctuary. He would select an armful of books, settle into an

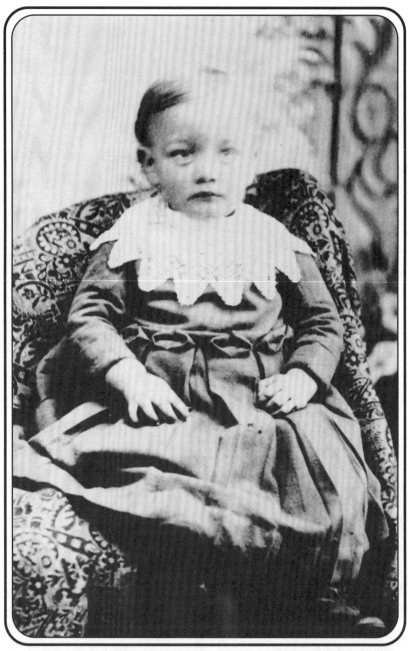

Howard Barnard, as a baby, showing he was "all-boy," with his right foot kicking. Boys were commonly attired in dresses for photos and formal occasions in the 19th century. (Photo, Barnard Library, LaCrosse, KS)

Howard Barnard at the age of two or three years. Barnard had exchanged his baby dress for high-top shoes, leggons [leggings], belt, bow tie, and hat. (Photo, Barnard Library, LaCrosse, KS)

easy chair, and read, totally escaping his physical surroundings and for-
getting his woes. Thus began a beneficial habit and pastime that lasted
throughout his life.

Barnard read the great philosophers and determined for himself at an
early age exactly how he would worship God. It would be in a rather
transcendental manner that would have made Ralph Waldo Emerson
proud. American Transcendentalists such as Emerson combined the
Unitarian religion in which they were raised with the new democratic
spirit of the land. In doing so, they created an intellectual religion based
on a belief of Nature as God as well as the divinity of each person.
Barnard also realized that it would be easy to study the heavens through
the library's skylight, and turned to the books to study astronomy, a subject in which he showed a lifelong interest.

Barnard cultivated this habit of self-improvement. On his own, he discovered that books were wondrous things that could explain the universe
surrounding him, as well as how the manmade things being used in New
York City worked. If childhood gives hints of the adult to be, Barnard's
days as a youth charted him perfectly.

It was there in those country surroundings more than in any school
that Barnard came to know the classical prose of Shakespeare and the
poetry of Keats, Shelley, and Milton. Yet he also displayed catholic
tastes with his great knowledge of simple nursery rhymes. And he especially liked the novels of Alexander Dumas, Charles Dickens, and Sir
Walter Scott. Barnard knew folktales, especially Aesop's fables, so well
that he frequently applied them to teaching situations throughout his life.

During his youth in New York City, Barnard once saw Ulysses S.
Grant drive his team of fine horses down a city street. From that time
forth, Grant was Barnard's greatest living hero, just as he was for many
other young people growing up at the time. Grant was a great soldier and
military leader, as well as president of the United States.

Barnard's childhood was filled with the usual 19th-century urban
experiences. Once while playing with other boys, he drove a stake into
the ground. A splinter chipped off and hit his eye, causing him to lose
sight in it. Luckily for him, he was in New York City and received such
good medical attention that the doctor was able to restore his vision after
nearly a year of treatment.

An adventurous side of Barnard manifested itself in one incident

Ulysses S. Grant, Civil War general and president of the United States. Grant was Barnard's lifetime hero. He had once seen Grant in a New York parade. (Photo, Library of Congress, Washington, D.C.)

when he was ten years old. He had arranged a hiking excursion for a three-day visit to relatives across town in New York City. After setting out, he spent a night at the Newsboys Lodging House, an orphanage funded by the various newspapers of the city for the many young immigrant children made homeless when their parents had died after the stresses of the hard Atlantic crossing. These young boys sold newspapers to survive. He found it more fun "hanging out" with the "stained urchins and orphans" and never made it to his relatives' home, much to the horror of his Victorian family.

A Chinese proverb states, "May you live in interesting times." Barnard, growing up in New York City in the notoriously corrupt 1870s, did just that. The city was already flooded with immigrants from Ireland, and many more would be arriving from other European countries, especially Catholics from Italy and Jews from Russia. To welcome them was a political machine thought by many to be the most corrupt of all time, Tammany Hall, controlled in the 1860s and early 1870s by "Boss" William Tweed. It was said that Tweed took millions of dollars from honest New York City taxpayers and stuffed them into the pockets of his notorious Tweed Ring. However, Tweed's organization supplied a need in the pre-welfare state and thus most of New York's indigent citizens voted for the ring who had welcomed them with a basket of food the minute they had set foot on the docks. The Tweed Ring kept its questionable dealings hidden for a long time, but finally, by the mid-1870s, Thomas Nast's political cartoons appearing in the *Harper's Weekly* seemed to stir people to take action. While Tammany Hall did not fade away, "Honest John" Kelly replaced Boss Tweed as its leader in 1872. Kelly also profited from Tammany, but at least he cleaned it up.

As Barnard grew up in New York City, he also experienced the city's tremendous physical growth. Ironically, this was mostly outward, not upward. It would be only after Barnard had left the city at the start of the 20th century that New York's famous mile-high skyline developed. During Barnard's youth, the tallest structures were the many church steeples.

Undoubtedly, the most interesting construction project of Barnard's boyhood was the Brooklyn Bridge. The raising of this bridge was, in many ways, symbolic of what New York City was becoming and what Barnard would later come to reject — a large metropolitan area. During

To Barnard, during his boyhood in New York City, one of the more fascinating projects was the construction of the famous Brooklyn Bridge. (*Harper's New Monthly Magazine*, May 1883)

Barnard's time there, the only way to travel from the island city to Brooklyn was by the colorful ferries. If New York City was to connect all of its communities, it would need a faster system of transportation. To this end, German-born John A. Roebling had designed the Brooklyn Bridge. He died before the bridge was built, but left the plans in the very capable hands of his son, Washington A. Roebling, who later became an invalid as a result of the bends he had experienced making frequent trips into the bridge's tower caissons that were not properly pressurized, by today's standards.

The Brooklyn Bridge was completed in the spring of 1883. It was an architectural wonder for its time, having the longest span of any bridge in the world at its dedication on May 24. Today, it is still functioning and is considered one of the most graceful bridges to view. It connects Brooklyn, in 1883 the third largest city in the United States, with its giant partner, New York City. The bridge provided foot, horse, carriage, and rail traffic to thousands of Greater New York citizens. But its con-

Henry Barnard, Howard Barnard's famous great-uncle. This portrait was done by F. Tuttle in 1886 when the great-uncle was 75 years old and had retired to his native Hartford, Connecticut. (Photo, Connecticut Historical Society, Hartford)

struction was just another sign to Barnard that city life was not for him. One year before it was finished, Barnard decided to head for Kansas.

Another invention that changed New York City and would later be pioneered by Barnard in western Kansas was Alexander Graham Bell's telephone. Bell had demonstrated it in New York City in 1877. Two years later, the nation's first telephone exchange had opened in the city. While Barnard relished the new inventions of the Gilded Age, he did not like the demographic changes taking place in his city of birth. He felt there were simply too many people for him and that they were the wrong kind. The Russian Jews, with their thick accents, seemed as threatening as had the Roman Catholic Irish and the Italians. There was no indication that Barnard held particular racial, ethnic, or religious prejudice; he simply believed that a more austere, maybe even pastoral, life among white, Anglo-Saxon Protestants was more to his liking — and Kansas, even though it was in the "wild" West, was less crowded.

Henry Barnard

Many youthful experiences influenced Howard Barnard's later life. But to fully appreciate or understand Howard, one must know of his relationship to his great-uncle, Henry Barnard. In the course of his upbringing, Howard Barnard spent several winters with Henry in Hartford, Connecticut. Howard realized just how prestigious his great-uncle was when he and several companions got into trouble and punishment was not meted out to him as it was to the others. This difference in treatment, Barnard thought, was morally wrong. Why should someone have greater privilege than another simply because he was related to an influential person? This injustice stood out in his mind and was a factor in his moving to Kansas later in life, partially to avoid the stigma of a name of privilege.

Living with Henry Barnard, Howard found more structure than with his parents in New York. He spent each evening at home. The elder Barnard sat at one end of a large table as the younger one did his homework at the other. At precisely 9:00 p.m. each evening, lessons were concluded and it was time for bed. When one winter evening Henry Barnard discovered that Howard's handwriting was exactly like the textbook examples, he enlisted Howard to copy articles sent to him that later found their way into his *American Journal of Education*. This journal was the first truly national periodical in the field of education and was an enduring monument to Henry Barnard's lifetime work in the profession.

Two people are often associated with America's first and most lasting education reform effort, the Common School Movement: Horace Mann, who has an elementary school in many cities named for him, and Henry Barnard. The Common School Movement is a term applied to the widespread effort in the United States ante-bellum period of 1820-1860 to bring conformity to the many one-room country schools and two-room city schools. This conformity, accomplished state-by-state, involved the textbooks, curriculum, number of school days, teaching methods, and length of each school day. Although Mann was the evangelist for the Common School, Henry Barnard remained its more solid scholar, especially through his writings and the editing of his educational journal. Connecticut led other states in its zeal for school reform, probably because of the influence of Yale University and the strong Calvinist religious fervor throughout New England.

The movement that some considered a "revolution" for school improvement began in the 1820s and did not stop until the Civil War. Henry Barnard became a leader in the reform movement because of his educational preparation and knowledge.

Henry Barnard was born at Hartford, Connecticut, into the Chauncey Barnard family, in 1811. He had a happy boyhood characterized by perfect attendance at "Sabbath" school in the Congregational Church and regular attendance at a public school, South District School. At an appropriate age, Henry Barnard was sent to Monson Academy in Massachusetts by his father because he was fearful that Henry was plotting to run away at sea. Henry did not last long at Monson. He returned to Hartford Grammar School, a highly prestigious school that gave him a classical education. Just before his 16th birthday, in January 1826, Henry Barnard entered Yale College. He loved Yale and returned as often as possible following his graduation, rarely missing a class reunion.

Uncertain about what to do with his life after graduation, Henry accepted a schoolmaster's job in a small Pennsylvania town, but he was anything but successful in this endeavor. He hated the school building, the town, and what he claimed to be the "dirty" Pennsylvanians. He became so irritated that he quit in the middle of his tenure.

For the next few years, Barnard did only two things — he read and he traveled, mainly in the South, with an extended stay in Washington, D.C. He returned to Hartford in the mid-1830s, believing he had to make a decision either to stay in Hartford the rest of his life or to head West to begin a new one. He chose the former. Still young and single, he studied at Yale Law School and became interested in the international peace movement. In 1835, he sailed with a friend, Herman Humphrey, to London as a delegate from the Connecticut Peace Society to his first international conference. The six weeks of sailing influenced Henry Barnard in a variety of ways. Through conversations with Humphrey, Barnard became increasingly convinced that in education lay the real hope of reforming mankind. Once in London, he took tea with Thomas Carlyle, Scottish essayist and historian, and John Stuart Mill, British philosopher and economist. Mill was considered by many to be the most brilliant man of his generation in the first three-quarters of the 19th century. He was certainly a product of enlightened thinking and would have influenced Barnard to consider a school curriculum based on ubiquitous reading, particularly history and literature, including poetry and that most practical of all intellectual exercises, writing. In addition, Henry Barnard undoubtedly identified with Thomas Carlyle's great appreciation of family and family duties, for Carlyle's father had sacrificed nearly all of his family resources to give him an education. At the age of 14, Carlyle walked 90 miles to enroll at the University of Edinburgh. Later, he sacrificed to help his brothers with their schooling. Barnard was impressed with Carlyle's beliefs about education being the means by which society not only trains its leaders, but selects the most honest and able. To Carlyle, and to Barnard, the character development of each student was the most important lesson. It was a necessity for every good teacher to embed values into the curriculum of reading, writing, and arithmetic, as well as into all other subjects.

Perhaps the trip to the conference was merely an excuse to travel abroad, for Henry Barnard was far more impressed with his travels to Scotland and to the European continent than he was with the peace conference. He also traveled extensively in Ireland, Germany, Italy, and Switzerland. One biographer contends that Henry was on a mission to visit the great educator Johann Pestalozzi, in Switzerland. At that point in his life, however, Barnard may not yet have heard of Pestalozzi; in addition, Pestalozzi had been dead for nearly ten years! In later years, Barnard did make Pestalozzi a household word in the annals of the Common School Movement.

Barnard returned to Hartford, still without a well-defined mission for his life. He had passed the Connecticut bar in 1834, and officially became a lawyer.

Drawing on his legal background, he campaigned and won election to the Connecticut state Legislature in 1837. A major accomplishment there was his successful sponsorship of a bill to provide better state supervision of all Common Schools. In fact, this bill changed his life. He abandoned the peace movement for another one — to universalize education throughout America, starting with Connecticut.

Barnard was re-elected to the state Legislature in 1839. But more importantly for education, he was appointed secretary of the Connecticut Board of Commissioners of Common Schools. In this capacity, he suggested that the state needed to better train its teachers. One way to do so was to establish a Normal School. In the United States, these were modeled after the French *ecole normale*. They were two-year institutions that provided teacher training for students as young as 13 or 14, immediately out of elementary school. The curriculum consisted of courses in philosophy and history of education, teaching methods and ideas, and "demonstration" teaching. In the 19th century, Normal Schools provided one of the few opportunities for women to receive a higher education. Later, in the early 20th century, our teacher colleges evolved from them. Barnard said that if they could not establish a Normal School, the least they could do was to bring teachers together for a week to attend a course of study on school methods and governance. Years later, Henry's great-nephew, Howard, would advocate the same in western Kansas.

Henry Barnard also appreciated the importance of public libraries. He founded the earliest library connected with a Common School in Connecticut. He also was first to propose legislation taxing citizens in order to establish community public libraries. He offered to give a certain number of books for a library to any district that would establish a school, thereby connecting schools and libraries. He praised New York's school library system and regretted that Connecticut had none. Furthermore, as a stop-gap measure, he recommended that a traveling library be placed in each school district, contained in heavy cases, and circulated among schools.

As secretary, he also founded and edited the *Connecticut Common*

School Journal, in 1838. As would be the case in his *American Journal of Education*, published later, Henry Barnard emphasized greatly the superior educational development of the countries of Europe. One of his early publications contained an article about education in China. He envisioned the American Common School Movement as eventually affecting the entire world.

In 1842, Democrats gained the majority in the Connecticut state Legislature. They abolished Barnard's position of secretary to the Board of School Commissioners, saying that it had only been an experiment in school governance and that the experiment was over. Barnard became just another Whig politician out of work — but not for long.

Henry Barnard moved next door to Rhode Island in 1843 and was appointed by the governor to serve as the official assessor of education. At the time of his appointment, Rhode Island's educational system consisted of small dame schools (one-room schoolhouses run by a schoolmistress), a few village schools, one collegiate-level Latin grammar school, and a few tutors. School finances came solely from donations. Much work needed to be done, and Barnard was just the person to do it.

Barnard began his transformation of Rhode Island's educational system with a series of town meetings. He outlined a system of Common Schools for each town, which began with a neighborhood elementary school, to be followed by a middle school; he even proposed a high school for each. He firmly believed that these schools should be open to students of both sexes and that their goal should be to prepare both boys and girls for useful lives. Barnard criticized teachers for "experimenting" on community children. Barnard's reason for criticizing the quality and methods of teaching was that he wanted to implement Normal Schools to train teachers in some of the modern methods with which he had familiarized himself in Europe. Howard Barnard had not yet been born when his great-uncle gave these Rhode Island town meeting speeches. However, the model for Henry's proposed community school was one that later became near and dear to Howard. Once in Kansas, Howard incorporated these ideas into his Entre Nous School, established shortly after the turn of the century.

By one account, Henry Barnard made over 1,000 speeches in his attempt to start a Common School system in Rhode Island. A point of contention and resistance by the people was that of financing — schools were simply too expensive. Barnard countered that argument by stating that schooling was much cheaper than the alternative — the later costs of pauperism and crime resulting from ignorance. Some ideas about the justification of education seem to remain eternal!

By 1844, Barnard was ready to take on the Rhode Island state Legislature on behalf of a major education bill. In it, he proposed a state system of schools, administered uniformly by a superintendent. Following the bill's passage in 1845, the governor convinced Barnard to accept the position he had helped to create. For four years, until his health failed, Barnard served the Rhode Island people admirably, particularly the school children. Perhaps his greatest legacy in Rhode Island was the Institute of Instruction he had established to train the teachers he had accused of doing such a poor job.

Henry Barnard's Rhode Island years were not all work, however. In 1847, he married Josephine Desnoyers, whom he had met on a trip to Detroit, Michigan. The marriage between a French Roman Catholic and a Puritan New Englander turned out to be a surprisingly happy one, blessed with five children.

When Henry Barnard resigned his Rhode Island post, Yale College tried to establish a professorship for him in the department of philosophy and arts. However, the position was never endowed. He declined professorships in history and literature at other colleges, as well as school superintendencies in Boston, New York, Cincinnati, and New Orleans. Indiana University and the University of Michigan each elected him president, but he declined both offers. Fortunately for Barnard, he was from a family of substantial means and could afford to do whatever he wished.

For the next few years, Barnard remained active in educational endeavors by chairing several national committees and attending an international educational convention in London. In 1850, he accepted the superintendency of the Common Schools in his native Connecticut. Perhaps more importantly to him, he accepted a joint appointment as principal of Connecticut's first Normal School located at New Britain. In his first year, Barnard enrolled and trained 55 students for positions as teachers.

During the decade of the 1850s, Henry Barnard gave particular credence to many of the women teacher-educators of the time. He was, perhaps, the only professional educator to do so. He published articles by Emma Willard, founder of Middlebury Female Seminary, later Troy Academy in Troy, New York; Catharine Beecher, who founded the Hartford Female Seminary in Hartford, Connecticut, as well as the American Women's Educational Association; Zilpah Grant, one of the founders of teacher education in the country; and Mary Lyon, founder of Mount Holyoke Female Seminary, now Mount Holyoke College, in South Hadley, Massachusetts. He also published their biographies and gave their work wide coverage. Barnard believed that women were "uniquely endowed by the Creator" to enter the profession of teaching. He believed that women had the intellectual capacity to teach just as men did and that they were better prepared to nurture children than those of his own sex.

In 1858, Barnard accepted the chancellorship of the University of Wisconsin, which soon became the least happy experience of his long career in education. Barnard seemed unconcerned that the university was in desperate financial straits because of fiscal mismanagement. But failure to attend to such details would later lead to disastrous consequences for his nephew, Howard Barnard, in Kansas. Henry Barnard, at the time, was more interested in the development of the Normal School duties of training teachers than he was in developing the liberal arts and sciences programs of the university. By 1861, his health once again failed him, and he resigned his post and moved back to Connecticut. While some of the faculty resented him, others praised his advocacy of a strong public education. Barnard had apparently recovered from his "nervous prostration" by 1866, for at that time, he accepted the presidency of St. John's College in Annapolis, Maryland. However, he was ineffectual in this post. St. John's College had closed during the Civil War, and Barnard's job as a Northerner was to revive this Southern institution. As he traveled across the state seeking financial and moral support, he found little of either. In 1867, the United States Congress spared him the embarrassment of resigning by appointing him Commissioner of Education. He thought this was a position that he was much better prepared to handle.

As America's first Commissioner of Education, Barnard said that this was the only job he would ever "turn on his heel" to acquire. He had been advocating this national position for 30 years. The Constitution of the United States makes no mention of education. Although the issue had been debated in Philadelphia in 1787 at the Constitutional Convention, the founding fathers decided that education was one of the items that was best left to the states. However, both Henry Barnard and Horace Mann believed that this was a major omission, and at every turn they had campaigned for a national department of education. They had even gone so far as to suggest that it should be included in the bill that established the Smithsonian Institution back in 1847. Barnard and Mann concluded that education was based on science and art, just like the Smithsonian.

In 1854, the American Association for the Advancement of Education did approve a resolution that had one unifying strand. It stated that in some way the federal government should interest itself in the education of the whole people. Although the Civil War seemed to stop the movement for a federal agency, the National Education Association and the National Association of School Superintendents continued to support its establishment. James A. Garfield of Ohio, later president of the United States, finally sponsored a bill establishing a National Bureau of Education. With a few changes, the bill passed Congress and was signed into law by President Andrew Johnson on March 2, 1867. Two weeks later, Henry Barnard was appointed the Bureau's first commissioner.

The specific charge of the agency has changed little over the years. It was to collect school statistics in each of the states and to diffuse information that might help schools organize and manage their systems, as well as to suggest better teaching methods. Barnard went to work immediately. He directed the most comprehensive inquiry of one nation's schools that the world had ever seen. He demanded to know everything about the administration, instruction, and management of elementary schools, colleges, professional and special schools, charitable and reformatory institutions, and societies for the advancement of education. He solicited information on school funds, legislation, architecture, and documents, as well as memoirs of teachers and other benefactors of education. At the end of one year's time, he presented his findings to Congress in an 881-page report.

Most members of Congress did not understand the function of the Bureau of Education. Consequently, every appropriation hearing was a major battle. Barnard, who was not particularly adept at budgeting, had a difficult time explaining his department's mission and justifying its spending. An unprincipled clerk who acted as an informer to Congress hampered Barnard's every effort, undermining and discrediting Barnard. On July 20, 1868, Congress abolished the Bureau and replaced it with an Office of Education. Barnard stayed awhile longer, but his heart was not in the job. He became indignant and resigned in 1870. An ex-Army general was appointed by President Ulysses S. Grant to replace him.

Undoubtedly, Barnard was partially to blame for his demise as first U.S. Commissioner of Education. When he had accepted the position, he was extremely popular and was considered to be an expert on education in this country. But upon assuming office, he became dictatorial, even in his relations with Congress. Success in the position, as he visualized it, was practically impossible. The office had very limited resources for Barnard's grandiose plans. Nationally, he believed education was in a chaotic state. Northern elementary schools had suffered severely during and after the Civil War. The few schools that had existed in the South had been completely demolished. Western states needed much aid and advice that could not begin to be provided by Barnard and his staff of two.

For the last time, Barnard returned to Hartford, Connecticut, never again to serve in a public office. In all probability, it was at this time in the early 1870s that Howard Barnard came to live with his great-uncle. Henry took up writing a history of education in Connecticut and resumed publishing his *American Journal of Education*, first begun in 1855.

For a long time, educational historians considered Henry Barnard to be the first educational editor and his *American Journal of Education* to be the first publication of its kind in American educational journalism. However, Edith Nye MacMullen, in her excellent revision and reinterpretation of Henry Barnard's life and works, has demonstrated that these were not "firsts." To Barnard's credit, he had always given credence to others before him who had attempted to publish a national education journal.

Nonetheless, Barnard continued to publish his *American Journal of Education*, uninterrupted by the trappings of public office, until 1881. The first few volumes in the early 1870s were practically almanacs of Barnard's 30 years in education. Then, in 1876, Barnard began the *International Series* in his *Journal*, because he believed that Americans were becoming too nationalistic in their outlook.

In his later years, Barnard remained alert and interested in educational concerns both locally and nationally. Barnard was a lifelong man of
letters. He was both an avid reader and a writer — a connection not lost
on his great-nephew, Howard Barnard.

Another concept not lost on Howard was his great-uncle's idea of
libraries. Henry Barnard was a lifelong collector of books. At age 12, he
began to buy books. He said that from a very early age he had seen as an
aim in life the gathering and disseminating of knowledge. Like so many
young men in early American times, college libraries disappointed
Barnard because of their inadequacies. In fact, fraternity libraries were
usually better than college libraries, hence an academic reason to join a
good fraternity. When Barnard had attended Yale, he had soon discovered that as an underclassman he did not have access to books in the
library at all. Barnard joined Linonia, the debate society, in large part
simply to use their library. It was not long until he had become assistant
librarian.

After graduating from Yale, Henry Barnard had become president of
the Hartford Young Men's Institute, established primarily to provide a
library for its members. He assembled 5,000 volumes to open its first
reading room. Barnard also wrote a history of Connecticut's libraries in
his *American Journal of Education*. He concluded that towns with
libraries produced more college graduates and citizens who were better
informed because they read more newspapers. This led to a better community spirit.

In his first report as secretary to the Connecticut Board of
Commissioners of Common Schools in 1839, Barnard had pointed out
the lack of school libraries. With missionary zeal, he had advocated the
necessity and great advantage of having such libraries. He was always
quick to compare Connecticut's backward ways in this area to forward-
thinking New York. In 1839, Barnard had tried in vain to get the
Legislature in his home state to appropriate funds for school libraries.
When that failed, he had offered to donate books from his own collection to any district school that would start a library. Several districts took
him up on his offer. Barnard believed that many times young people
could learn more from reading a book than from some of their teachers.

When he had headed the Rhode Island schools in 1843, Barnard had
succeeded in obtaining 500 volumes for 29 of the 32 school libraries. He

had also advocated public libraries as zealously as school libraries. He printed a listing of public libraries in principal states, capitals, and universities of Europe in an attempt to get the United States to follow their lead.

When Henry Barnard died in 1900, he left behind a personal library of over 10,000 volumes. Fortunately, financier J. P. Morgan, railroad mogul and founder of United States Steel Corporation, donated the money to preserve the library in the Wadsworth Athenaeum on the Trinity College campus in Hartford. A few of the books became part of Howard Barnard's personal collection and found their way to the high plains of Kansas. They are now housed in the library that bears the famous Barnard name in LaCrosse.

Learning later that Howard Barnard was related to people of wealth and power back East did not surprise the uncomplicated but perceptive folks of western Kansas. They had a shrewd way of analyzing strangers in their midst and had sensed something unusual, yet important, about Henry Barnard's great-nephew.

Kansas-Colorado Exposition Building at the 1876 Philadelphia Centennial. Howard Barnard was so impressed with the exhibits in this building that he vowed to go West to Kansas. (Photo, Kansas State Historical Society, Topeka)

Chapter 2

The Westward Trek

If you have no family or friends to aid you
And no prospect open to you there
Turn your face to the great West
And there build up a home and fortune.
— Horace Greeley

*B*ELIEVING that a child's place was in school, Howard Barnard's parents, Harriet and Chauncey Barnard, III, did not take him with them when they attended the grand opening of the Centennial Exposition in Philadelphia on May 10, 1876. But because of their stories of its grandeur, young Barnard knew that he must see it for himself. He turned to his great-uncle Henry, who consented to take him and his brother to Philadelphia during the summer once school was no longer in session.

The interior of the Kansas-Colorado Exposition Building. A major part of the Kansas exhibit at the 1876 Philadelphia Centennial was agricultural produce arranged as the nation's capitol building. In the background is the Atchison, Topeka and Santa Fe Railroad exhibit that was also a part of the Kansas exhibit. (Photo, Kansas State Historical Society, Topeka)

The Centennial Exposition was opened in an election year by President Ulysses S. Grant as a celebration of the 100th anniversary of the signing of the Declaration of Independence. The Liberty Bell was once again rung in Philadelphia to mark its grand opening. Fifty other nations joined the United States in what was to be America's first world's fair, although it was not billed as such at the time. The exposition had 167 buildings, which covered 236 acres. It was a spectacle attended by over 10 million people. Certainly for its time, especially to a 13-year-old boy, it was every bit as impressive as Disney World is today. The main exhibition building at Fairmount Park included working models of every conceivable new machine, including many by Thomas Alva Edison. Displayed was a continuous web printing press that produced 1,000 papers per day; a farm implement called the self-binding reaper; the typewriter; the telephone; refrigerated railroad cars; and the Westinghouse air brake. Ironically, while the Centennial Exposition was supposed to be a celebration of the Declaration of Independence, its primary author, Thomas Jefferson, was greatly overshadowed by tributes to George Washington, which were literally everywhere to be found. One was an Italian sculpture that had Washington perched on an American bald eagle much too small for him. Of all the exhibits on display, young Howard Barnard was most fascinated by the Kansas-Colorado exhibit, which consisted mostly of the flora and fauna of the two states, along with advertisements that portrayed the West as being the new land of opportunity not only for farmers, but for anyone. This exhibit was especially attractive to the many Easterners who were in the midst of an economic depression at the time. The invitation, along with Horace Greeley's admonition to "Go west, young man, go west!" was not lost on Barnard. He remembered Kansas from that day on.

Five years later, in 1881, when Barnard was 18 years old, he bid his family good-bye and headed West on foot, quite literally. He rapidly discovered that Kansas was much farther than he had originally estimated. He had grown tired of walking that first day, and at dusk he was just coming to a small town when he was treed by a large brown dog. He fastened himself securely in the fork of the tree and spent the night. The next morning, Barnard headed north in order to go west, although this was not as illogical as it might seem. Following the Hudson River to Albany, New York, he planned to catch a ride — and employment — on

To help pay for his way westward, Barnard worked on the Erie Canal as a mule driver. (*Harper's Weekly*, February 22, 1873)

the Erie Canal and at last start his trek westward. Barnard had left the family mansion with no means of financial support. His family neither understood nor supported his interest in the American West; they had promised him a college education if he would stay in the East. But Kansas was by this time a fascination upon which he had to act. Barnard's plan was to work his way West by taking a job as a mule driver on the Erie Canal.

The Erie Canal was America's first important manmade waterway — so important that some historians have claimed it enabled the North to win the Civil War. The canal freed the upper Midwestern states from their dependence upon the Mississippi River as their outlet to the ocean, and hastened the industrialization of the North, contributing greatly to its accumulated wealth.

Work on the canal had begun on Independence Day 1817, just three days after DeWitt Clinton took office as governor of New York after campaigning on the platform of building a canal with state money. The canal was 40 feet wide, 4 feet deep, and 363 miles long, as the old song said, "from Albany (actually Troy) to Buffalo." It was the greatest engineering project undertaken to date in the United States and was partially funded through a New York state lottery. While some, including President Jefferson, believed it to be a "harebrained" idea and called it Clinton's "Big Ditch," Governor Clinton had the last laugh when it was completed eight years later in October 1825. The canal had cost a little over $7 million and was immediately profitable. By the time Barnard worked his mules along its shores in 1881, it had made over $121 million for New York state — reason enough to lift tolls the following year. Economically, the canal reduced the time and cost of shipping farm goods from the upper Midwestern states to the Eastern seaboard cities. The price of a ton of grain shipped from Buffalo to New York City fell from $100 to $5, and the time of transit was cut from 20 to 6 days. The canal allowed New York City to replace Philadelphia as the nation's premier seaport. Upper Midwestern states such as Indiana, Illinois, Ohio, Michigan, and Wisconsin gained numerous immigrants interested in farming their rich lands, since farming was more profitable because of the new route to the Atlantic Ocean. Many of the Irish immigrants who had been hired to build the canal had subsequently decided to move to these Midwestern states. Western frontier cities such as Cleveland,

Chicago, and Detroit began experiencing amazingly rapid growth. The Erie Canal proved to be an essential bond between East and West.

Barnard's job as mule driver was one of the essential jobs on the Erie Canal. Barges sometimes as long as 80 feet were towed by lines attached to teams of mules that walked along the shores of the canal under the control of the drivers. Travel was quite slow. Horace Greeley, the famous editor of the *New York Tribune*, remarked that passengers traveled a mile and a half an hour for a cent and a half a mile. Nonetheless, travel, whether passenger or freight, was steady. The canal provided employment for many young men such as Barnard. One mule driver on the Erie Canal, James A. Garfield, would later become president. Barnard could not have been acquainted with Garfield, as Garfield had worked on the canal during an earlier time. It is unclear whether or not Barnard worked even one round trip; it is likely that he did not. Barnard had stated later that he had learned to swear while working on the canal, as the only words the mules understood were curses, something apparently rather foreign to Barnard's strict Yankee upbringing.

After finally reaching Buffalo, Barnard hired out as a deck hand on a freighter westbound on Lake Erie. His naiveté about life in the working world led him to call attention to himself. He said, "If I had been smart I would have let the [ship's] officers hunt for me just as the other deckhands did." By the time the freighter reached Cleveland, Ohio, his hands were blistered from shoveling coal from the floor to a bin above his head and from scrubbing decks. He decided that this was enough waterfront experience to last him a lifetime.

Even though Cleveland was not his intended destination, he disembarked. He pushed farther southwestward into central Ohio, where he went to work for a farmer named Jack Shepherd. Some days he worked in the wheat fields and on others he would hoe rows of corn. A highlight for workers was the cook's dinner bell calling the field hands to come to the farmhouse to wash up for the meal. The work was only seasonal, and when it was over, Shepherd was kind enough to take Barnard to a nearby town and recommend him for a job as a grocery store clerk. Barnard said later that this job was the most confining one he ever held. He compared it to being a dog chained to its kennel. However, Barnard worked there for nearly a year, saving his money for the trip that would take him to Kansas. When he believed he had enough money, he once again headed West, this time following the railroad tracks. Walking on the tracks in Ohio, he happened to be in the middle of a railroad bridge over the Scioto River when he heard a train whistle. Realizing that he would be unable to make it to the end of the bridge in time to escape being run over, he crawled under the bridge and hung by his fingertips until the train had passed. On this trek westward, Barnard most often enjoyed good fortune, sometimes getting a ride in a horse-drawn wagon, and occasional food handouts — except in Indiana. He walked the entire distance across that state without a single offer of a ride.

In Illinois, he discovered a farmer who was getting ready to leave for Kansas along with two of his neighbors and their families. The farmer agreed to take Barnard with him in exchange for his labor along the way — gathering firewood and other odd jobs. The farm wagons were loaded, and the three Illinois families, along with Howard Barnard, left for Kansas.

After a day on the road with this caravan, Barnard could predict about how far it could travel; so he wandered off the beaten path daily to experience personal freedom and to enjoy the countryside. Each night he faithfully showed up to deliver on his promise of gathering firewood and tending to the chores. One night in Missouri, he approached the anticipated camping place only to find no one there. He sat down to wait for his caravan and fell asleep. The next morning, he was still alone. He began walking westward and came upon a farmhouse. The resident farmer informed him that the group he was looking for had passed his farm at midnight, stopping to buy eggs and milk. Barnard never saw these families again, although he had a vague idea of their intent to homestead close to the Colorado border in Kansas along the old Santa Fe Trail. Barnard tried his best to find them, trailing them over 300 miles to Kansas.

Although he said he did not record the date, he was quite sure that it was August 12, 1884, when he stood with one foot in Missouri and the other in Kansas just south of Kansas City. In all probability, Barnard was nine miles south of the confluence of the Kansas and Missouri rivers on the old Santa Fe Trail. In a month, he would be 21 years old. He must have been quite a sight, standing five feet, three inches tall and weighing all of 110 pounds, with reddish-brown hair, a beard reaching nearly to his waist, and large sparkling blue eyes. Imagine this diminutive,

God-fearing Yankee as he entered perhaps the wildest territory on the North American continent in 1883.

If Barnard had intended to follow the Santa Fe Trail, he had arrived three years too late, for rail lines by then had a monopoly on the commerce that once had passed along this famous route stretching from Franklin, Missouri, to Santa Fe, New Mexico. However, he was not too late to catch a freight train leaving Kansas City and, after 75 miles, he was on the Atchison, Topeka and Santa Fe Railroad, which had, in fact, replaced the trail.

Although Barnard was not a tourist in a "palace car," he must have enjoyed the scenery as he whirled along the iron trail. The wide, muddy Kansas River gradually gave way to bright smaller streams that flashed and foamed. Barnard undoubtedly noticed that the trees and hills were fewer and farther between, giving way to broad seas of prairie grass. Dotting this ocean of endless plains were quiet little white farmhouses built by industrious people who had overcome tremendous odds to eke out a living on these Great Plains. He could not possibly have missed something else he had never seen before — the immense cattle ranches. Kansas was where the beef hit the railhead.

While the main line of the A, T & SF railroad followed the old Santa Fe Trail into the Arkansas River Valley around Hutchinson, noted for its extensive salt works, Barnard was on a Santa Fe freight train that diverted at Newton and went south to what would become the largest city in Kansas — Wichita. There he hopped another freight train, which took him to another famous point along the Santa Fe Trail, the great bend in the Arkansas River. The old Santa Fe Trail had run through what is now the Court House Square in downtown Great Bend, Kansas. This is where Barnard got off the train, still looking for his former companions.

Believing that he was still not far enough west, Barnard began walking in that direction along a trail near Walnut Creek. He may have believed this to be the Santa Fe Trail, but he was wrong, for the Santa Fe ran southwest out of Great Bend, not due west like Walnut Creek.

Thirty miles farther west, Barnard came to a small settlement called Rush Center. Believing that he was just about to be reunited with the Illinois families, he continued past this small hamlet in a western direction. He passed through another small town called Alexander, where the caravan had been spotted. He took a good look around and decided that this High Plains territory looked very much like the picture of Kansas he had held in his head since that summer day with his great-uncle Henry at the Philadelphia Exposition: rolling hills of prairie grass, green valleys growing forage crops, and gardens near white, wooden farmhouses. And in his mind, the sky was always blue with beautiful sunsets. Finally he decided to give up the search for his former companions. He walked back to Rush Center. Although he did not realize it then, he would eventually make Rush County, Kansas, his home for the rest of his life.

Barnard came to Rush Center penniless. In some respects he was lucky to have his shirt, pants, shoes, and hat. Asking about the possibility of work, he was directed to a farm just south of town where some farmers were growing sugar beets. Barnard was hired to run a primitive sorghum press that turned the beets into molasses. The molasses was stored in large stone jars for the winter. This job lasted several months until all of the neighbors had finished using the press. Then late one afternoon, Barnard was paid in full by the farmers, and the job came to an abrupt end. Once again he took to the open road.

It was late fall, and the prevailing wind from the south (the term "Kansas" comes from the Indian word for "people of the south wind") had changed into a more chilling one from the north. Barnard headed into this wind, going through the county seat, LaCrosse. There he headed West once again. After traveling ten miles, night began to fall, and it became colder. The only shelter in sight was a new haystack in a field. Barnard burrowed into it like a mole and found himself well insulated. He soon fell asleep. What a surprise it must have been for him to awake the next morning and, looking out from his new bedroom, find the ground covered with snow.

About a quarter of a mile to the south, Barnard saw what looked like smoke coming from the chimney of a house. It appeared to be made out of rocks or some kind of stone. Walking toward it, he discovered that the house was made of sod, a mixture of mud and grass cut from the prairie in two-foot squares, baked in the 100-degree heat of the Kansas summer sun, and layered together like bricks. Some people referred to this sod as "prairie marble." Barnard had never seen such a construction. Knocking at the door, he was greeted by a farmer named John Fudge, a 53-year-old native Pennsylvanian who lived with his wife Catharine and ten children ranging in ages from 4 to 21. Barnard later recalled seeing four or five small children hiding timidly behind the farmer. He inquired about work, and Fudge informed him that he might be in luck, for a neighbor by the name of Michael G. Curry, just three miles to the east, was looking for a sheepherder. Curry's sons, Everet, 24, and Emmet, 18, had been doing the herding but had grown tired of the job; and there was some urgency in finding a replacement, or at least an assistant. John Fudge insisted that Barnard have breakfast with them, however, before going to the sheep ranch. When Barnard offered to pay for the meal, they refused his money, saying that in return they merely wanted his good will. Barnard remembered this and considered it a part of the true pioneer spirit of Kansas, neighbors helping one another.

Barnard found the Curry sheep ranch and was immediately hired. The ranch consisted of 320 unfenced acres. The congenial Southern family was from Virginia. Besides their two sons, Michael and Viney Curry also had living with them two daughters, America and Dell, ages 14 and 1, and two other small girls, Anna and Ida Pierson. But they gladly shared their home with him.

Little did Barnard know that he had arrived just in time to experience the blizzard of 1884, the worst to hit the Great Plains in two centuries. In fact, "blizzard" may have been a new term to Barnard. It was first used as a weather phenomenon by O. C. Bates, an Iowa newspaper editor, in reference to a storm on March 14, 1870. It has been used ever since to apply to a severe cold wave accompanied by high wind, sleet, and snow. Blizzards then and now are described as being some of the worst weather occurrences of the Great Plains, with wind-chill indexes frequently at 50 degrees below zero, conditions hazardous to animals as well as people. Buffalo, which are Great Plains natives, will face and head into a blizzard, whereas cattle and sheep run away from the north wind, as would any sensible human who might be caught in one. It is hard to imagine, but farmers going just from house to barn in a blizzard sometimes got lost and perished. Consequently, sensible farmers fastened a cord or rope to the house so that they could find their way back.

When the terrible blizzard struck western Kansas in late December, it literally took cattle and sheep with it. The following spring many Kansas cattle were found in both Texas and Oklahoma, some dead, some alive. The Curry family had only 12 sheep survive out of a heard of 128. Many Kansas ranchers were completely wiped out and left their homesteads, never to return. Following the blizzard, Barnard helped the Curry family gather up the dead cattle, cutting off their legs to be used as fuel in the absence of timber that winter.

During the fall and winter of 1884-1885, Barnard attended Star School with the Curry boys. Their teacher was Molly Edwards. Barnard became a kind of teacher's aide or helper and took a great interest in promoting spelling bees. At one point, he generated enthusiasm by putting up a $35 watch as first prize, which was won by Jesse Busick.

Sometime in the spring or summer of 1885, Barnard decided that his adventure on the Great Plains was complete, and he returned to New York City. Upon his return, however, he found the city and his family to be even more stifling than he had previously imagined, and he took a train back to Rush County, Kansas, in 1886. But this time a knapsack filled with books accompanied him.

Barnard took up where he had left off on the ranching frontier. He became a cattle herder at a salary of $8 a month. He was not to become a cowboy — a cowboy rides a horse; a cattle herder walks. Barnard never mastered riding a horse.

Ralph Wallace suggested, in an article appearing in *The Rotarian* (which would later bring Barnard a modicum of fame), that, as a cattle herder, Barnard conducted his first "school" for Kansas children. Wallace stated that "the school had the sky for a roof and tufts of buffalo grass for seats and desks." Wide-eyed pioneer children and cowhands alike would gather around him at midday when the cattle were quietly grazing. Barnard would open his magic knapsack and read to them from his books. He was likely the first formally educated person they had ever met. To say these people seemed to be hungry for knowledge was an understatement.

Even the most hard-bitten cowboys began carrying a book along as they rode. At most, Barnard may have had six cowhands and children as students. In the middle of the day when the cattle were quiet, they would gather on a high prairie swell where they could keep a lookout on the herd, and Barnard would teach these unlikely characters, as well as the children, how to read and write. Barnard inspired these cowboys with his passion for "book learnin'." He furnished them textbooks from his knapsack, and writing lessons were completed on wrapping paper from the grocery store in town.

As if the blizzard Barnard had experienced in December 1884 was not enough, another, equally devastating, occurred in western Kansas in February 1886. Once again, many Kansas ranchers lost their entire herds and thus their investment in their new homesteads. And once again many of them left Kansas. Barnard did not leave, but he did some hard thinking about continuing as a cattle herder.

Chapter 3

High Plains Teacher

Teaching is a field in which there is
much work to be done. New hands are
very impatient to do something. Here
is your chance. Will you do it?
— Howard Barnard
September 19, 1902

*O*NE month before he turned 25, Howard Barnard made the
biggest decision of his life — to become a teacher, not just a traveling minstrel-teacher to young cowboys on the range who would listen
to him, but a professional educator. On August 4, 1888, Barnard
received his Kansas Teaching Certificate. Years later, citizens of the
towns of LaCrosse and McCracken perpetuated the idea that he had
achieved the first set of perfect scores on the state teachers examination. Although some of the mythical tales surrounding Barnard's life

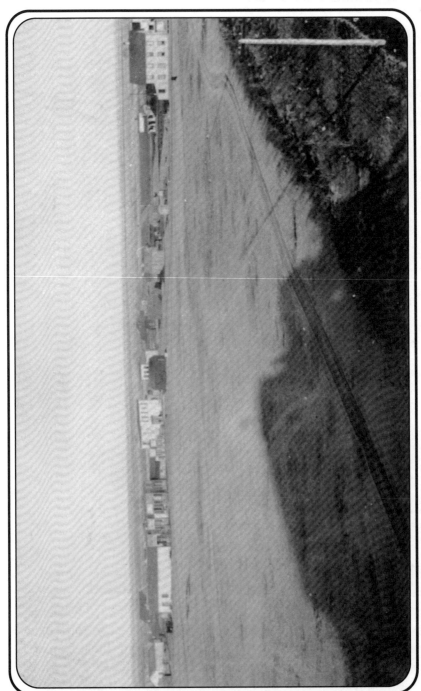

McCracken, Kansas, in the late 1880s, when Barnard first saw it. (Photo, Edith Chenoweth Collection, McCracken Public Library, courtesy of Carolyn Thompson and Shirley Higgins)

Barnard's half-brother, Philip Barnard, visited him in western Kansas while on his way to Colorado. (Photo, Barnard Library, LaCrosse)

were nearly true, this one was far-fetched. In fact, while Barnard had passed the test the first time with a respectable average of 92 percent, he had struggled with arithmetic and grammar, scoring only 50 and 61 percent, respectively. His highest score, and one of which his great-uncle Henry was undoubtedly very proud, was his 100 percent on the theories of teaching. Barnard also scored high in penmanship (95) and orthography, another name for spelling (87). His scores on the rest of the exam, which included reading, geography, history, and physiology, were slightly above average.

Over the next four years, Barnard continued to take the state teachers exam, improving his scores each time, so that he could claim high 90s or 100s in nearly every topic tested. Hence, the basis for the myth. In fact, he would improve his score in one area only to score lower in another. However, he never managed to get 100s in all areas in any one given year, proving that even sophisticated Yankees were not perfect!

Test scores aside (and they never have been a true gauge of teaching ability), Barnard was one of the best-prepared teachers on the Great Plains of America at the end of the 19th century. Barnard was a cultured man. Not only was he a member of an aristocratic family, but he had also lived a sophisticated life growing up in New York and Hartford. He had forsaken it all to begin a new career and a new life as a teacher on the High Plains of western Kansas.

This seemed sensible to those stout-hearted men and women who were already tucked snugly in their sod houses on the far Western frontier. In fact, very few in Kansas would argue that it was anything less than a highly intelligent decision, because New York was obviously suffering from what they considered "overcrowdedness" in late 19th-century Eastern America.

When school started in the fall of 1888, Barnard began his formal teaching career in a small, one-room schoolhouse known as Cottonwood School, located three miles northeast of McCracken, Kansas, in Rush County. It was named for a nearby group of trees bearing the name of the state tree of Kansas. Cottonwoods, while considered a soft wood, are hearty natives of Kansas, related to the poplars and aspens. In the fall, their leaves turn a beautiful golden yellow. They are majestic, often growing to 100 feet. Barnard, coming from an area where trees are plentiful, felt at home teaching in a school amidst those trees on the otherwise treeless Great Plains.

Barnard immediately became an educational authority in the small but growing community of McCracken. His services were in such great demand that the following year he received a better offer to teach in another one-room schoolhouse, Locust Grove School, which was over three miles north of Cottonwood School, making him nearly seven miles from the nearest town, McCracken. Locust Grove School granted Barnard the luxury of a salary for his services, unlike Cottonwood School where he had depended on the subscriptions paid by parents for their children who were his students. In November 1889, with only one year of teaching to his credit, Barnard began writing an educational column for the local newspaper, the *McCracken Enterprise*, which he continued off and on for the next 24 years. Once again, he was following in his great-uncle Henry Barnard's footsteps, as he, too, had been a journalist. Barnard wrote his column for the purpose of disseminating ideas

Barnard was 25 years old when he posed with his students in 1889 at the Locust Grove School. The newspaper that published the photo labeled him "a transplanted New Yorker and former cowherder." (Photo, Barnard Library, LaCrosse, KS)

about educational practice and theory to other teachers in the area and especially to parents, keeping them informed of school events and giving sound advice about their children. He began his first column with an untitled original poem:

> We think it is a rule, sir;
> To hate to be a fool, sir;
> And so we go to school, sir;
> To drive dull care away.
> There was a lazy Turk, sir;
> Who all his tasks would shirk, sir;
> He had no honest work, sir;
> To drive dull care away.
> But we propose to know, sir;
> And so to school we go, sir;
> To grow from head to toe, sir;
> And drive dull care away.

The Nichol homestead where Barnard had roomed when he took up teaching at Walnut Grove School in 1892. (Photo, Carolyn Thompson and Shirley Higgins)

This poem left little doubt about Barnard's philosophy of teaching. He aimed to instill in his students the Puritanical ethic of hard work, an ideal apparently lacking today throughout much of America, but still very much a part of the western Kansas psyche even at the end of the 20th century, over 100 years after Barnard put forth his educational ideals in the form of his poem.

Barnard continued to teach at Locust Grove School for the next two years. In 1890, he had 17 students and received $25 monthly for the six-month school term. In 1892, once again receiving a better offer, Barnard moved to a different school, Walnut Grove School. This one was two miles southwest of Locust Grove School and closer to the growing town of McCracken. Still, it was a one-room country school in every respect.

Barnard continued writing his newspaper column, becoming so bold as to criticize School Superintendent Hockensmith for insisting that each teacher in the county tack up a price list of school books for the next five years when the seller stated that the prices would go up every 90 days. The superintendent had met his match. Barnard also suggested that "the worthy superintendent" needed to get money raised to purchase equipment. Every time a school in the county would get a new piece of equipment, it was reported to Barnard, who publicized it in his newspaper column and suggested that every other school in the county should have a like piece of equipment. He was ecstatic when Cottonwood School bought a Webster's Unabridged Dictionary with stand, and when a colleague, C. H. Kuns at South Fairview, got a physiological mannikin, a globe, reading charts, and wall maps. Slowly, but surely, the country schools on the High Plains were becoming better equipped and modernized.

Although some schools enjoyed a few equipment advantages, every school on the plains adhered to a regimen that was uniform and over 400 years old — the curriculum, which was centered on the teaching of the 3Rs (reading, 'riting, and 'rithmetic) and the teaching method of recitation, whereby a student would read and then recite the reading to the teacher when called upon. These educational methods had come from England with the early colonists and had moved along the frontier in America. That type of country school teaching, which had occurred on the Eastern seaboard in the 1600s, was in evidence in the Mideast in the 1700s and in the Midwest in the 1800s. In fact, this model was still very much in evidence throughout the first half of the 20th century in the Midwest in sparsely settled farming areas. Even though teaching methods have drastically advanced, in 1980, there were still over 500 one-room schoolhouses in operation in the state of Nebraska. And these students, far from being deprived, scored much higher on standardized tests than their city counterparts.

But in 1890 in western Kansas, one could go into any one of hundreds of the country schools and at 9:00 a.m. expect to hear the Pledge of Allegiance to the Flag and watch the curriculum follow a precise order for the remainder of the day, even though there was not a state-mandated curriculum guide. Teachers seemed to carry a blueprint for teaching in their minds resulting from the way they had been taught. In addition, by the 1890s in Kansas, each county had elected a superintendent of schools who was to enforce such conformity.

Howard Barnard's school day began at sunrise. He typically lived with one of the nearby farm families. During his early years, he also lived in a dugout at one time, which was literally a hole in the ground; a sod house made of prairie marble; a house made of Kansas limestone quarried in the area; and a frame house. Each of these places of shelter was a far cry from the mansions of his youth. Each morning Barnard would walk the distance of a mile or so to the school well ahead of his students to build a fire, as the Kansas wind-chill dictated. The potbellied stoves in the early plains schools burned coal, if available, wood, or dried buffalo and cow chips. Barnard would sweep the floor with a mixture of sawdust and oil, clean the wash basin, and pump enough water from the well for the entire day. He was also responsible for maintaining the outhouses, which usually meant pouring lime down the holes and stocking toilet paper or a suitable substitute for those all-important detached buildings.

After the opening exercises — saluting the flag, reciting the Lord's Prayer, and reading the Bible — Barnard would begin the daily routine for his students with reading lessons. Mornings also included arithmetic and writing, as well as a 15-minute recess. Each student brought lunch from home, usually packed in a syrup pail, which looked much like a one-gallon paint can. Molasses spread on two slices of homemade dark bread was a popular sandwich, as were cucumber sandwiches in season. The food was typically starchy, but sometimes it included protein by way of farm-butchered/cured pork or beef sausage, or a piece of rabbit meat. Noontime also meant spending the remainder of the lunch hour outdoors for the therapeutic value of nature. Barnard would often join in a game of baseball or drop-the-handkerchief with his students.

The afternoon session usually began with Barnard reading some classic children's book to his charges, books like *Black Beauty, Tom Sawyer, Heidi, Robinson Crusoe, Treasure Island, Little Women*, and *Aesop's Fables.* Then lessons continued with grammar, history, geography, health, science, and spelling. Each afternoon session also included another 15-minute recess with school dismissing promptly at 4:00 p.m. Barnard usually spent another hour or two preparing the school and his lessons for the next day. Consequently, when he put on his jacket to walk home each night at around 6:00 p.m., he had put in a 12-hour workday.

Howard Barnard loved every minute of his work, because for him it was a labor of love, not only for his students, but for his country and for the betterment of mankind. He believed that by educating youth on the farming frontier, America would become a better place to live. This was

The Fort Hays-Fort Dodge Trail, the military trail connecting the two famous forts at Hays City and Dodge City. The trail crossed Big Timber Creek Bed just beneath the hill where Hampton School was located. Of the one-room country schools in which Barnard taught, Hampton was his favorite. This famous trail has recently been marked by a chapter of the Santa Fe Trail Association. (Photo, by Allan Miller)

not accomplished through some patriotic zealous activity, but rather by solid, quiet, Yankee persistence.

* * * * *

If Barnard affiliated with one country school more than any other, it was the Hampton School, located on the military road known as the Fort Hays-Fort Dodge Trail. Hampton was a "wide spot on the trail" that included a school, a general store, and a post office. Today a cemetery and a trail marker are the only remaining signs that this was once a town. In 1893, Howard Barnard taught 32 students at Hampton for a 7½-month term. That year, the big excitement in Barnard's life and in that of many of the children and parents in the Hampton community was the opening of the Cherokee Outlet land in Oklahoma. The *McCracken Enterprise* carried articles as early as February 3 about the possible passage of the Peel Bill by the United States Congress, which would open additional Indian territory in Oklahoma to white settlers. The federal government would pay the Cherokee nation more than $8.5 million over 6 years at 5 percent interest for 6.5 million acres of land around the 98th parallel in Oklahoma. This was land that was leftover after individual Indians had had a chance to claim it. As noted in the *McCracken Enterprise* of July 28, 1893, any man or woman head of a family who was at least 21 years of age and was a citizen of the United States of America could enter a homestead of 160 acres provided he or she had not already enjoyed the benefits of a previous land stake elsewhere in the United States. Each homesteader would have to pay from $1.00 to $2.50 per acre, depending on the land's location, the farthest west being the cheapest. The homesteader was to secure the land first, then file for it later, although other possibilities existed. Whole towns could be laid out and established for $10 per acre.

Howard Barnard was approached by his friend, Frank Start, about joining him and his brother Al, John and Joe Whorton, Chris Derr, and Tom Hall in a trip to stake out claims, but Barnard said he had no interest in the venture. So without him, the men from McCracken headed south in their wagons. The first night they camped just south of Bazine, Kansas (about 20 miles from McCracken). Around two in the morning, they heard someone calling their names. When they answered, Howard Barnard walked into camp, lucky to be alive because of the commotion he had caused. He had walked to join them because he had decided that "someone had to stay in the tent and take care of the money and I was the only one who didn't drink." Frank Start agreed to let him ride in his wagon along with the Whorton boys.

On September 16, 1893, just two days after his 30th birthday, Howard Barnard was poised to take part in the greatest land rush in American history, the Cherokee Strip Run. That morning, the McCracken men raced after their land on horseback, but failed to secure any. Barnard and John Whorton, who had no horses, caught a ride in an old wagon from a stranger who knew the territory; he took them quickly to two unclaimed quarter sections of land.

Cherokee Strip Run. On September 16, 1893, Oklahoma land was once again opened to those who could get there the fastest from Kansas. Edna Ferber celebrated the run in her book, *Cimarron*. Barnard claimed land in the run, but gave it away within two days and returned to Kansas. (Photo, Kansas State Historical Society, Topeka)

After the run, while many were wandering around waiting to file for their land, Howard Barnard called Frank Start out of a saloon and told him that he could have his quarter section. Barnard had no real interest in developing a farmstead anywhere but in Kansas. Start declined the offer, but said that he would wait in line with Barnard to help him file. However, growing impatient with the long line, Barnard attempted to give his land to Chris Derr, but he, too, refused. Finally, Barnard asked Frank and Chris for $5.00 so that he could return to McCracken, using as his excuse that school was going to begin soon at Hampton and that he had a great deal of preparations to make. They loaned him the money, and Barnard walked back to his prairie home, passing through Wichita where he spent $3.50 of the borrowed $5.00 for a book. He walked over 200 miles to return to his home.

Once home, Barnard decided that the Hampton School was too small for his 32 prospective students, so he singled-handedly built an addition on to it 12 feet long, which became the student cloakroom. Barnard also

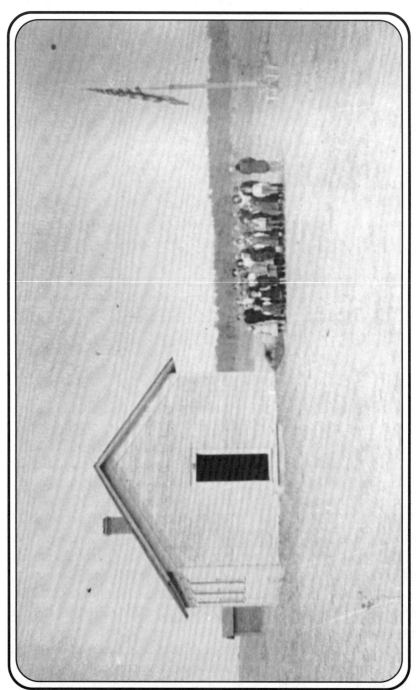

Barnard with his students some time in the 1890s at Walnut Grove School. He gave the school its flagpole, believing it was the obligation of every teacher to present some gift to the school and community. (Photo, Carolyn Thompson and Shirley Higgins)

built an addition to the Star School, located a few miles southeast of McCracken, where he later taught — and perhaps to several others as well. At both the Hampton School and the Star School, Barnard spent his own money to purchase the lumber. He also used his own money to buy the Hampton School a large bell that could be heard for nearly two miles — the first bell in any of the area schools. Throughout the ages, teachers have subsidized their classrooms because of their love for the children and their desire to provide the best possible education for them. Barnard was no exception.

A highlight of each school year for Barnard and his students was the Christmas season. Barnard obtained a cedar tree from a farmer in the area who had cut it from a stand called Cedar Bluffs, which grew along the banks of the Smoky Hill River, 25 miles north of the Hampton School. Barnard decorated the tree with precious fruit and his schoolroom with stars, planets, and a crescent moon, just in case Santa Claus should lose his way in the jollity of the season on his way to Hampton School. As he had done in years past at other schools, and as he was to do in schools later in his teaching career, Barnard packed the house for his Christmas program. He directed the children's glee club in the singing of Christmas carols, many of the students gave special readings, and there was a gift exchange among the students. According to Barnard, a typical complaint of the parents was that the program was too short. Barnard's curious wish for the parents of his students was that "they have a pocket full of money and a cellar full of beer" — curious, because he was a self-proclaimed teetotaler.

It was also in 1893 that Barnard gave up his newspaper column in the *McCracken Enterprise*, perhaps because he had so many students for such a long school year. He channeled his energies into lesson preparation and other teaching duties and did not resume the newspaper column until January 8, 1897.

In 1895, Barnard changed schools again, returning to Walnut Grove School for a two-year period before becoming the schoolmaster at Brown School in 1897. Brown School was nearly 10 miles northeast of McCracken, the farthest from town of any of the schools in which he had taught. Barnard received $27.50 a month for a six-month term there, which was $2.50 more than the previous year at Walnut Grove. Wherever he worked, he insisted that the school board treasurer divide his monthly salary and give it to him in weekly installments, forcing him to budget more carefully and relieving him of the need to carry much cash on his person.

During this period, Barnard was active in two main causes. He started an area teachers organization — the McCracken Teachers Association — and he became an active leader in a county summer Normal Institute, which trained teachers in the latest teaching techniques. Barnard enjoyed the considerable socialization that these institutes offered. He had first participated in a Normal Institute as a leader in the summer of 1895 at LaCrosse, Kansas, the county seat of Rush County. Although his motive in starting the local teachers organization is uncertain, he said that it was because rough weather would prevent area teachers from going all the way to LaCrosse to attend the county teachers organization meeting in the winter. He also candidly suggested that there was a "shining cluster of schoolma'ams in the woods around McCracken to have a lively time."

The McCracken Teachers Association would go several months without meeting; then it would meet biweekly for four months. A typical meeting was several hours long and consisted mostly of program content rather than business. It would open with a song, followed by several recitations and formal papers, a lecture, discussion, miscellaneous business, and a closing song. Barnard either presented a paper or gave the main lecture. He appeared to love instructing teachers as much as or more than he did students. Barnard later became president of the teachers organization and was a permanent fixture at the county teachers Normal Institutes for the next 20 years. He was an early advocate of the professional development of educators as well as the betterment of students through the professionalization of the discipline. He was practicing what his great-uncle Henry Barnard had preached for years, back in Connecticut.

While Barnard was teaching at Walnut Grove School in the winter of 1896, an interesting event took place, one that developed into a local legend, which every native son or daughter of the area for nearly three generations could tell a stranger. It concerned Barnard's feet. As one can imagine, the story had several different versions! Some said that Barnard had frozen his feet as early as 1884 in one of the worst blizzards of the century while he was a sheepherder. Others said that it happened when

The Ben Hicks Ranch, 1889, the largest cattle ranch in Rush County, Kansas, when Barnard arrived near McCracken in the late 19th century. (Photo, Jack Wilson)

he walked to Hays, 25 miles away, or to Topeka, 200 miles, or to Denver, 300 miles, to buy books. It was a fact that he had walked or hitchhiked to each of these cities on occasion, and that he was a cowhand in the blizzard of 1886. Any of these trips or events could have led to his feet being permanently numbed from repeated frostbite, but pictures seem to indicate that it was not until 1897 that he began using the felt boots that were to become his trademark for the rest of his life.

That year, Barnard and 20 other guests were invited to a New Year's Day dinner at the home of Mr. and Mrs. Felt Derrick of McCracken. The guests pleasantly passed the day by fishing, singing around the piano, eating, and talking. It was a memorable experience for Barnard, who spent the night with the Derricks. On the next day, which was a Saturday, Barnard started walking back home, only to get lost after "floundering around for some hours through sloughs too numerous to mention, carrying a sack of oranges and candy." Even without snow on the ground, Kansas wind-chills can be 40 below zero and can cut to the bone. Luckily for Barnard, he was found by the Rush County "cattle king," Ben H. Hicks, who took him to his ranch, warmed him up, kept him

Barnard's famous boots, which were actually boot liners made of Russian felt. (Photo, Allan Miller)

overnight, and got him to his own home the next day. Barnard had suffered frostbite, but was otherwise fine.

Whether or not it was suggested by Hicks is uncertain, but Barnard subsequently purchased a pair of felt boots and accompanying rubber outer boots from the J. M. Hastings Store in McCracken for $2.00. These boots actually looked more like boot liners. They were originally made in Russia for the cold winters there, but High Plains cowboys, ranchers, and farmers quickly realized their utility. Most of these hearty Kansas folks owned a pair of the calf-length boots, which were then protected by rubber outer boots. To say the least, the boots were well insulated and stayed dry until the outer rubber boots developed holes. By then it was most likely time to replace the felt portion as well.

Barnard wore only this type of boot for the remainder of his life, claiming that they were the only thing that felt good and that protected his frozen feet. He later discovered that these felt boots were also perfect for librarians to wear, as they were quiet. He wore rubber slickers over them only until he reached his school or library, then removed them while he was inside, rather like the old Dutch or Japanese customs of leaving one's shoes at the door.

Students and other library patrons soon became accustomed to Barnard puttering around in his felt boots. One can deduce that such footwear had to be replaced every year, since he was scooting around with them on a hard, yellow pine or oak floor. It is also altogether possible that Barnard wore them for "effect." If so, one might speculate that in the 100-degree, "hotter than blazes" Kansas summers, he might go barefoot — a practice he apparently avoided. When his felt boots wore so thin that he was almost barefoot, he cut out shoe liners from cardboard and stuffed them inside his felt boots to get a little more mileage from them before buying a new pair. The last pair of felt boots he owned before his death are on display in the Barnard Library in LaCrosse.

Barnard began his second decade of teaching in western Kansas in 1898 by changing schools again, his sixth school (not including a summer stint at the Fairview School in 1897). This time he was at Pleasant Hill School, located 20 miles southeast of McCracken and 2 miles east of LaCrosse. Barnard took a slight cut in pay to teach there at $25 per month. One could speculate that something in the community was not quite right for Barnard to have moved farther away from his beloved McCracken. Possibly he just realized that he had devoted ten years of his professional life to the area and simply wanted a change, although some would contend that going from one side of a western Kansas county to another was not much different. At the time, Barnard's mother, whom he had worshipped, was in poor health; on October 14, 1898, in Hartford, Connecticut, Harriet Barnard died. It is not known if Barnard's move to the Pleasant Hill School was in anticipation of his mother's death, perhaps an attempt to isolate himself from the community at McCracken, which he knew so well.

After having a year to accept the death of his mother, Barnard decided to return to the McCracken community. His decision to leave Pleasant Hill came after two controversies had occurred at the school. At a literary society meeting on March 16, 1899, Barnard had conducted a ciphering match (math contest), which he himself proceeded to win.

Howard Barnard at Pleasant Hill where he taught in 1898. Here, with his "black beard," he posed with his eight charges. (Photo, Carolyn Thompson)

Although teachers often entered these contests, on this particular night, it was the manner in which he had won that had caused the dispute. There was a misunderstanding about one of the conditions — namely, whether the points were to be divided by the number of nights of the contest or by the number of nights a contestant participated. Barnard thought everyone understood that the points were to be divided by the number of times each person took part and demanded in no uncertain terms that because it was his school, that was the way it would be. Consequently, he won. If the points had been divided the other way, Otie (Leota) Jennings would have won.

On another occasion, Barnard had a bright male student who was extremely good at arithmetic, so he challenged the Whitehead School to a ciphering match. Believing that his student could not be defeated, he offered his own fine pocket watch as the prize. However, his star student was defeated by Faye Jennings, of Whitehead, and Barnard refused to give the watch to a girl. These two controversies and Barnard's handling of them were talked about for years.

It was probably fortunate that Hampton School called him once again as its teacher in the fall of 1899. He was to have his biggest class to date — 33 pupils. He would be paid $33 a month, which represented a 75 percent increase in his pay. Additionally, the term was for seven months, one month longer. If there was one school that could be considered Barnard's, it would be Hampton, where he taught ten years in all.

Barnard resumed writing his *McCracken Enterprise* newspaper column during the years 1897 through 1899, sometimes writing lengthy essays concerning corporal punishment (not specifically banned by Kansas law until 1991), which he was against. He pointed out that Kansas law supported him by stating that if a school teacher stooped to the use of the whip, it was illegal to leave a mark on a student. Barnard preferred instead to simply expel an unruly pupil, for he felt that it was a disruption to the other students who had the right to learn.

Barnard also embraced the great good that he said came from a liberal education and believed that it was necessary to combine as many subjects as possible into the Common School curriculum, such as those he and others taught in country schools. He wrote that the Greek Xerxes had discovered long ago that the kindness and courage of human beings came from the power of united action. Barnard understood this to mean that knowledge had to be combined and connected in order to be useful and, therefore, good. Barnard believed that this liberal education on the farming frontier of western Kansas was far superior to the education that children were getting in the cities across the United States. He felt that the countryside was purer and the people were heartier and, in a way, more intelligent and wiser. Barnard was only one of thousands who believed in this rural Populism. His contemporary, William Jennings Bryan of Nebraska, had campaigned for the U.S. presidency on these very tenets and was barely defeated in 1896.

Most of Barnard's newspaper columns during these years, however, were devoted to school announcements, attendance figures, and good-natured hints:

Our good looking school board is practicing some of their

New Year resolutions. This time they have stuck up notices for a special meeting to consider an addition to the school term. That is right, gentlemen!

By the turn of the century, Howard Barnard had promoted himself as the leading educator in Rush County, if not all of western Kansas, through his newspaper column, his growing reputation, and the innovative ideas he was trying at Hampton School. By 1900, he had accumulated 34 weeks of attendance and assistance at county Normal Training Institutes and 300 weeks of teaching experience.

Perhaps in order to enhance his reputation even further in the area, Barnard, in 1901, once again changed schools. He selected Star School five miles southeast of McCracken for his teaching experiment that year, receiving an increase in pay to $50 per month. Some people have called this the "Start" School, because Barnard attended it when he lived with the James K. Start family and because some of the Start children were students there. However, this is incorrect; it was the Star School.

During the two years that Barnard taught at the Star School, his life-long interest in collecting and sharing books increased. That first summer, he set up a reading room for teachers attending the Normal Institute in LaCrosse. He was given the upstairs northeast room in the Rush County Courthouse for this purpose. The room was open during the daytime institute hours for studying and became the social center for the attending teachers at night, thanks to Barnard furnishing it with his own gas lanterns and his Crown organ. The newspaper reported that his library study or reading room was a "howling" success. Barnard had purchased the *International Cyclopedia* and the *Century Dictionary* for $100 each. His generosity did not go unnoticed. The teacher "normalities" were grateful for Barnard's valuable service and tireless efforts in support of their profession. They passed a resolution that stated:

We make special mention of the kindness of Professor Barnard [he had never been called Professor before] in giving us access to his valuable books and study room and for his personal help in the preparation of lessons.

During these years at Star School, Barnard was struck with a serious

At the Star School, baseball and physical education were always an important part of Barnard's curriculum. It was at Star School that he first used the term "Entre Nous." (Photo, Marie Brack)

illness in May 1901. This malady, which could best be described as stemming from emotional causes, was to haunt him, as were his injured feet. Today, we might be inclined to label it as "burnout." Barnard literally worked himself into such a frenzy that he became nearly dysfunctional. He termed his spells "brain fits."

At this time of his life, Barnard met Edith Miller, a fellow teacher who taught at Elm Grove School, also in Rush County. If Barnard, the quintessential bachelor, felt love for one woman other than his mother, it was Edith Miller, a good-natured, extremely competent, attractive woman whose company he enjoyed immensely. He would later employ her and work with her at his own school.

The concept of starting his own school was the fourth significant circumstance to emanate during this time at the Star School. Barnard had enlarged the school, and people had frequently joked with him that it would be cheaper if he simply built his own school to his own specifications to start with. The idea was planted. At Star School, the students had been divided into two study groups, each with a secret name, which the other tried to guess. Only the initials could be given as clues. During the 1902 school year, the groups' initials were ENS and FCB. No one knows for certain what FCB represented, but according to Barnard, ENS stood for Entre Nous Society, *entre nous* being French for "among ourselves — between us." At the turn of the century it was a popular phrase. Reading circles, church circles, and women's clubs were so named. Nevertheless, Barnard like the sound of it so much that he gave that study group a prize for the best name. Later, he would use it as the name for his own school.

Barnard decided to start his own Normal Institute to train teachers. His plan was to hold a one-month institute immediately after the school term was finished near the end of April 1902. This institute would enable some of his Star School eighth-grade graduates, who might be interested in teaching, to take a prep course before going to the Rush County Normal Institute in June. For this month of training he would charge $1.00.

Barnard placed an advertisement in the newspaper stating that he would be assisted by three area teachers, two women and one man, who were chosen because each used entirely different teaching methods. Students would be allowed to choose their instructor in order to match their instructional style. Interestingly, some contemporary teachers think this concept was first developed in the 1980s!

Barnard advertised a curriculum for his Normal Institute that included 16 different subject areas, among them German, bookkeeping, and psychology. Additional attractions, he noted, would include a Crown organ, baseball, croquet, tennis, a pool table, a tent, and 100 combination games. This pre-Normal Institute, to be held at Star School, was called Professor Barnard's Entre Nous School, and he had 16 students.

During the Christmas vacation in December 1902, Barnard was filled with excitement as he boarded a train for Chicago to purchase (with his own money, naturally) an x-ray machine for his school. Every big city high school at the time had one, and a surprising number of country schools had purchased them as well. So Barnard, ever eager to bring the finest ideas to the frontier schools, went to Chicago to make sure the piece of equipment he purchased was the finest available and that it functioned properly. This massive x-ray machine, built by two Germans named Toepler and Holtz, weighed in excess of 500 pounds. Barnard sometimes referred to it as simply "the apparatus." It was used not only to demonstrate x-rays, when an electrode tube was attached to it, but to teach magnetism and electricity, as it could generate 600,000 volts. However, without electricity in rural schools prior to the 1930s, this machine had to be turned manually to generate its own power in order to operate.

Upon Barnard's return from Chicago, once again he could not complete the county Normal Institute training the following May, because of illness. He thus retreated to the countryside to recover before school started in the fall. Either because of this illness, or for some other unknown reason, Barnard once again changed teaching positions, returning to Hampton in the fall of 1903. Hampton had offered him the same $50-per-month salary that he had received at Star School. Hampton would have the advantage of Barnard's bringing along his x-ray machine, as well as his 300 books, which would provide a rather formidable library for a country school.

During these early years of the 20th century, and perhaps *because* it was a new century, Barnard changed the name of his newspaper column from the rather plain title of "Educational Column" to the lofty "Under the Stars." It quite possibly could have been a play on words of the Kansas state motto, *Ad Astra per Aspera*, "To the Stars through Difficulties."

In 1904, Barnard once again signed a contract to teach at Hampton School. His school library had grown to 700 volumes. However, unfortunately for the students that year, the school had to be closed in December because of a smallpox epidemic. Nonetheless, Barnard was full of sage advice in his newspaper columns. Imagine being a new teacher on the High Plains of Kansas at the turn of the century, opening the *McCracken Enterprise* to Barnard's column and reading:

> In every school you teach try to leave something tangible behind to remember you by. Have trees planted. A library commenced. Real slate blackboards put in [many High Plains blackboards were merely black paint offset with white boards for trim]. A fence about the grounds. A United States flag floating from the school house. A school organ in the house. Scrapers at the door. Hitching posts erected. A natural history cabinet started. Remember that a step taken in the right direction is sure to be followed by others. The first step is the hard-

est and each succeeding one is easier till that which was first only a pleasant dream is an accomplished fact. The road to success is gained by hard work. I say, there is much to be done. Will you do it?

These were not hollow words from some Eastern theorist; these were words that were practiced by this wonderfully innovative Yankee on the prairie.

Chapter 4

The Country School Legacy

Our one-room country schools
Have all but faded away
Like those soldiers of yesterday
Our noble rural teachers

What fun those good times must have been
Wonder if they'll come again?
Yes, I think that I recall
They do, every Fall
— Allan R. Miller

Early Schools

THE famous American humorist, Will Rogers, a product of a number of one-room country schools, was fond of saying, "School ain't what it used to be and never was." The most sentimental image in American education is the one-room country school. For a major part of his life, Howard Barnard lived, breathed, and helped create that image, which is widespread because it spans both time and space throughout every part of the United States. The nation sprang from rural roots. To meet the educational needs of a rural nation, Puritans in the 17th century levied taxes and established one-room schools, which were called district schools because of the taxing district that best defined them.

As Puritan offspring pushed into the backwoods of Pennsylvania and the Ohio Valley, they established schools because the Northwest Ordinance of 1785 provided aid to education. This ordinance predated the United States Constitution, adopted in 1787 and put into effect in 1789, and stated that throughout all newly surveyed lands in the country, section number 16 of the numbered acreage was to be reserved for education. These law-abiding American citizens interpreted this ordinance literally. They either erected a school on section 16 or sold it and used the profits for educational purposes. It should be no surprise to anyone that the schools created in the 18th century looked and sounded much like those of a century before.

As civilization advanced into the Great Plains states like Kansas, and the 18th century gave way to the 19th, one-room country schools on the High Plains still resembled those Puritan district schools of 200 years earlier.

Although separated by many years and many miles, these one-room country schools symbolized the American commitment to the betterment of its society. Not only would American society improve by wiping out illiteracy through the teaching of the 3Rs, but also by teaching strong core values like punctuality, responsibility, honesty, and, as Barnard said over and over again, hard work.

Midwestern country schools performed this two-pronged task perhaps better than schools in any other section of the country. Today, education surveys show that the Midwest contains the most literate people in the United States. More importantly, there is no better example of participatory democracy in the American saga than the establishment and operation of one-room country school districts. One can logically contend that this pattern continues today with the control of most school matters still in the hands of local school authorities known as school boards of education.

In our late 20th-century mindset, country schools take us back to simpler, more peaceful and serene times, when problems, educational and otherwise, were less complex and more easily solved by a hero on the order of Almighty God or the Virgin Mary — the country schoolmaster or schoolmarm.

In late 19th-century America, there were over 200,000 one-room schoolhouses, 8,000 in Kansas alone. A majority of Americans still lived in rural settings, but not for long. The 1920 census confirmed that a majority of Americans had elected to move off of the farm and into villages and cities. However, in 1930 there were still nearly 150,000 one-room schools, comprising the majority of elementary schools in America. Especially in the Midwest, country schools were in their heyday. How in the world did these schools come about in rural Kansas and the rest of the Midwest? Quite simply, they followed the pattern that was first suggested in the Northwest Ordinance of 1785.

The Rise of Midwestern Country Schools

As soon as land in Kansas was surveyed and laid out in sections of 36 square miles constituting a township, farmers purchased the land, many times from railroads, and began turning it into the "breadbasket of the world" by carefully planting and then harvesting each June their hard, red winter wheat. The sale of section number 16, reserved for educational purposes, gave each township a pool of money to be used to create rural school districts. Each of these newly created school districts incorporated about six square miles of land, with the one-room schoolhouse to be placed in a central location so that children did not have to walk more than two or three miles each way. Sometimes before the school could be built, children were instructed to meet with a teacher in such places as the former saloon, if they were in Larned, Kansas, or in a cave, if near Kanopolis.

In 1858, the Kansas Territorial Legislature provided for the election of a three-person school board to establish and oversee the development and implementation of each local school district. These boards were all male, for, in the thinking of the time, educational administration was too important to be left to women, although in Kansas females were considered superior to males as teachers because of their motherly traits. Each school board member was elected for three years. One was the chair, another was the clerk, and the third and most important was the treasurer. Their job was to build the school, maintain it, supply it, and hire a teacher as cheaply as possible.

In many instances, the erection of a one-room schoolhouse was the first community business in a newly settled area. Once the school was completed, it was used for a variety of purposes, including religious worship services (sometimes Methodists would meet on Sunday morning, Baptists in the afternoon), weddings, funerals, elections, farmers' union meetings, and lyceum programs. Several of the latter in late 19th-century Kansas were debates on whether people who could not read and write the English language should be allowed to vote. This was an especially sensitive issue in Kansas communities such as Lindsborg, with its large number of Swedish immigrants, and Hays, with an equally large number of Volga-Germans.

The usual number of farm families that supported a school district was 20. If each of the families averaged four children, two of whom were school age at any given time, a teacher would have her hands full with 40 children ranging in age from 5 to their mid-20s, in some cases. The teacher was responsible for teaching grades one through eight in the same room.

Criteria for Country Schools

Once a site for the school had been established and a fireguard plowed around the site as a barrier to protect it and the children from the frequent prairie fires, residents tackled the questions of how big the school should be and what it should be made of. When Howard Barnard decided to teach on the High Plains of Kansas, most of the schoolhouses there and throughout the Midwest were no more than 30x50 feet and were built from whatever native material was available. Because the High Plains was devoid of trees, early Kansas settlers used prairie marble, or sod. Sod homes and schools were made by layering pieces of earth cut in 4x4x14-inch brick-like sections. As one might imagine, the roofs on these buildings needed constant repair.

Just as plentiful as sod and much better for school construction on the treeless plains was the uniformly thick-layered white or yellow limestone. All over western Kansas, "rock chalk" one-room schoolhouses dotted the countryside. By 1930, it was not unusual for a western Kansas county to have over 100 of these schools in operation at the same time.

In eastern parts of Kansas and other Midwestern states, log and stone schools gave way to the more sophisticated wooden frame "little red" (or white) schoolhouses and then to brick buildings as America entered the 20th century.

Throughout the Midwest, as Normal Colleges were created to train teachers, professors from these colleges lobbied farmers to pay close attention to the building of their schools. In Kansas, at Fort Hays Normal, for instance, shortly after the turn of the 20th century, the Manual Arts Department stated in a bulletin that its members would gladly draw plans free of charge for any school board that wanted a truly model school. In fact, the Department built a model rural school on the campus and conducted classes in it. Department members tried to get farmers to quit building the old-fashioned box school. They believed it was time to consider comfort of children, beauty of construction, convenience for teaching, and sanitation. They showed that a sod school in Finney County near Garden City was much improved by being built from adobe — something not usually done in Kansas.

Early professional educators were concerned that the school yard needed to be large enough to accommodate a game of baseball that did not interfere with playground equipment. They were not concerned about the closeness of the school to new roads, called highways, for the safety of children, but rather for the appearance of the building to people as they rode by.

The recommended size of a school building was at least 24 x 32 interior feet to house 40 students, based on 16 square feet of floor space and 200 cubic feet of air space per pupil. This meant that the school would need 12-foot ceilings. Farmers were cautioned that higher ceilings meant considerable heating lost from the potbellied stove.

Windows were to be banked together as closely as possible to give the effect of one large window, what we would call today a picture window. Curiously, these early education professors recommended placing windows all on one side of the building. This would prevent cross-shadows as well as eyestrain on the part of students, which was thought to produce nervous disorders later in life. However, for purposes of ventilation in warm weather, one or two windows could be placed in the rear of the schoolhouse on either the north or the east. Each of these windows was to have a good canvas shade.

A new consideration for the early 20th-century schools was to place screens over each window and door to keep insects, especially flies, out of the schoolhouse. On the Kansas plains, screens could also prevent window breakage from hail.

Normal School professors not only encouraged school boards to purchase durable real slate blackboards, but, in addition, "nothing but the best dustless crayons need be used" — the less dust floating through the classroom air, the better the health of the students and teacher. Blackboards were to be placed 28 inches from the floor to allow small children access. They needed to extend high enough so that all students could see the assignments. Under no circumstances should the blackboards be placed between windows, which would lead to unnecessary eyestrain.

In most one-room country schools, wall colors followed the recommendations of the experts of the time and were painted a light blue-gray or green. Many teachers believed that light green led to better student creativity, an idea that carried into late 20th-century urban schools with their "institutional green" classrooms. Because ceilings diffused light from the windows, they were left natural, if wooden, or painted a lighter color than the walls.

The early country schools simply provided coat hooks in the back of the room for children's wraps in the winter. But Normal School professors pointed out that this was wrong. A separate cloakroom for boys and for girls was advisable to overcome the unsightliness of the situation, as well as to promote self-respect and respect for the school building. Often in rural schools, wraps were simply piled on unused desks, creating a sanitation problem that did not meet with the approval of the Normal School experts.

The few books of the country school were kept in homemade bookshelves. Many were purchased by the teacher as a gift to the children. Howard Barnard made a major case in his newspaper articles, as well as by example, for teachers to keep purchasing books, including dictionaries and encyclopedias. Gradually, at the urging of Normal School professors, these few books provided by the teacher gave way to small libraries purchased by the school boards. These were sometimes assigned a special corner of the schoolroom, separated by partitions.

Much sentiment lingers for the country school's "old oaken bucket" that, along with a single cup or long-handled pitcher, was shared by the students and the teacher. By the turn of the 20th century in the Midwest, the oaken bucket was replaced by a metal one. Because of advances in bacteriology, Normal School instructors suggested that the reason one student came to school with a cold and the rest of the children caught one may have been the sharing of the same water bucket, cup, and pitcher. If a school was fortunate, it had its own water well. If not, water was hauled in, sometimes from as far away as a quarter of a mile. Children, in these cases, were deprived not only of fresh water but also of clean water. Fort Hays Normal professors suggested that school yard water wells could be improved by pumping water with a windmill all year long. Pumping water in the summer when school was not in session would guarantee pure water in the fall when school resumed. They suggested digging a few irrigation ditches and planting trees around the school, reducing the waste of the constantly flowing water.

In the earliest country schools, split logs, known as puncheons, were placed around the walls to answer the need for student seating. Later, straight-back, stiff-seat, double desks were used. Double desks were interesting for their educational as well as physical properties. Students could learn their lessons cooperatively and at the same time learn something about the value of sharing space and books, as well as ideas. These desks gave way to curved-back, folding-seat, single desks by the turn of the 20th century, patented by such companies as the Empire Seating Company of Rochester, New York. These new desks were shipped by train to the High Plains of Kansas.

Single desks were made to be permanently screwed to the floor or onto runners in single rows. The front of each row was left with a seat only, which served as the recitation bench for students waiting to recite to either the teacher or the entire class.

Fort Hays Normal education professors believed and suggested that single desks were best for learning, but that they should not be screwed permanently to the floor. They believed each desk should foster the independence of each student as a complete unit in itself — and it was less disturbing to others who wanted to learn. The professionals also wanted single desks that could be adjusted for the size of the pupil and that had a storage drawer for books and personal articles, which could be locked beneath the seat. These desks had the advantage of promoting cleanliness, as every inch underneath could be swept. They could be arranged in any desired manner for social purposes and for lighting and heating conditions of the school, and their number on the floor could be decreased or increased as the number of students necessitated.

Also important to rural students was physical exercise; thus morning and afternoon recesses were held each day in addition to noontime outdoor games and play. Early playground equipment included swings and teeter boards. Later, as country schools became more sophisticated, or school equipment salesmen became sharper in their practice, playground pieces such as merry-go-rounds and giant slides became commonplace.

Also prominently decorating the school yard grounds were the outhouses, usually separate ones for boys and girls. R. L. Parker, an associate professor of education at Fort Hays Normal, called the outbuildings in western Kansas schools disgraceful and said that they too frequently contributed to filth, as well as vulgar imaginations, referring to the sayings on their inside walls. He found most of them to be "merest makeshift" and a breeding ground for flies. They were certainly offensive to both eyes and nose. He recommended treatment by chemicals, as well as septic-tank closets. He was especially fond of one called the Kentucky sanitary privy devised by the Kentucky State Board of Health for schools and farms in that state.

As school district budgets would allow, pictures, maps kept in wooden cases, and school clocks decorated the interior walls. The most popular pictures were those of presidents Washington and Lincoln, usually high above the blackboard at the front of the classroom on either side of the clock. Some schools had a place for a mirror and wash basin, often with old sardine cans for soap trays holding some of "grandma's lye soap."

School Days

Throughout the Midwest, while the traditional 3Rs dominated the curriculum, nine subjects were universally taught: reading, writing, arithmetic, agriculture, history, geography, grammar, orthography, and physiology. The three main textbooks that dominated the country classroom were the *McGuffey's Readers*, *Webster's Spellers*, and *Ray's Arithmetic* books. Lessons in reading, writing, spelling, history, grammar, orthography, and sometimes agriculture and geography all could be taught from *McGuffey's Readers*.

Indeed, the *McGuffey's Reader* was a type of Western civilization book of virtues. It consisted of a set of six graded readers (the first in America) to be used for students from grades one through eight, although the number on the outside of the reader did not equate with the grade in which the student matriculated.

The *Reader* began like the *New England Primer* it replaced, with learning the alphabet, but soon got into morality plays where good little boys won competitions and bad little boys always lost and were punished. Little girls were taught that their rightful place was in the home or at least doing women's work.

William Holmes McGuffey used poetry and prose from the most prominent Western writers, as well as from Shakespeare and Long-fellow. However, the Holy Bible was the most frequently quoted source. The Victorian ideals of hard work, literacy, and virtuous living were espoused by McGuffey quite naturally, as he was a clergyman nurtured in the values of Scotch Presbyterianism.

More than 150 million copies of *McGuffey's Readers* were sold between its original publication in 1836 and 1930, and it is still in publication today. Its popularity in the early part of the 20th century can be traced to Henry Ford, the automobile industrialist. Ford admired McGuffey, probably because of his propagation of hard work for the American labor force that Ford had to draw upon for successful automobile production. Ford's acknowledgment that he owed his personal success to *McGuffey's Readers*, and his philanthropic endeavors in purchasing these readers for schools, ensured McGuffey's place in educational history in this country. Ford preserved McGuffey's home and school for posterity by having them moved from Ohio to Michigan, where they are on display in his Greenfield Village in Dearborn.

The teaching and learning method in the one-room schools focused on recitation and memorization. Students were given assignments to read, write, and memorize. When they completed them, they came forward for their recitation session beside the teacher's desk on the raised floor area that was "teacher territory." Sometimes students would invade this territory in small groups (with the teacher's permission) for cooperative recitation. These small groups usually consisted of all the students in a single grade. The country school was probably not as quiet as some-times thought, considering the variety of assignments that needed to be given to eight different grades, and the amount of recitation that had to be performed almost continually. Students and teachers sometimes used small slate boards. On occasion, students were called forth to diagram sentences, construct maps, or write out math problems for others to see on the slate blackboards. When Big Chief Tablets replaced individual small slates, teachers could have students hand in assignments for later grading.

Perhaps the most practical teaching method in rural schools was the peer tutoring that took place. It was expected that the older students would assist the teacher in listening to younger students recite, as well as actually helping them master spelling and math, and other assign-ments. The peer tutoring was not just any older student helping any younger student, but older siblings helping the younger ones where pos-sible. This certainly fostered the strong sense of family responsibility characteristic of Midwestern rural life. Some professional educators today believe they have found evidence that older students helping younger ones stimulates greater learning — something that occurred in country schools to great advantage for over 100 years.

Respite from the normal rural school routine sometimes came on Friday afternoons with enjoyable competitions in the form of spelling bees and ciphering (math) matches. Sometimes the teacher would even take part by being on one "team" or the other, while one of the older children served as "headmaster" or pronouncer. At other times, Friday afternoons were spent on art or craft lessons.

One characteristic of country schools experienced by all children was the games that were played. In Kansas, where the winters were mild in comparison to the upper Midwest, a rare snowfall led to students mark-ing out large circles in the school yard for a game of "Fox and Geese." Perhaps the most popular of all children's games was "Hide and Seek." However, on the treeless plains of Kansas, there were not many places to hide, so other games became popular, such as "Annie High Over," a game played with two teams and a ball. Teams would be out of sight of one another on either side of the schoolhouse. One team would yell "Annie High Over" and throw the ball over the roof to the other side. If someone from the other side caught the ball, that team would tear around the schoolhouse to tag some member of the opposing side. If the ball touched the ground first, that team would in turn yell "Annie High Over" and throw the ball back. The side having the most players at the end was declared winner. "Capture the Flag" was a popular boys' game, along with marbles and baseball. Girls played "Jacks" and "London Bridge is Falling Down," along with jumping rope.

Howard Barnard and other teachers conducted lavish Christmas programs that involved all families of a school district, but the most important country school program was the end-of-the-school-year extravaganza usually held the last of April. This was a celebration primarily for those eighth-grade students fortunate enough to have passed the county Common School examination. The day consisted of games, great food, and a student program. By the 1920s, many counties had county-wide graduation ceremonies held in the county seat. These events were perhaps more significant in the lives of the country school students than high school baccalaureate ceremonies are today. An eighth-grade education was nothing to sneer at!

Eighth-Grade County Exams

In Kansas, the county eighth-grade exam first appeared in the 1870s. Originally it was not mandated by the state but was prepared on the local level by the superintendent of schools, or by appointed examiners, from books such as *Stephenson's Kansas State Eighth Grade Question Book*. The book consisted of 108 pages of open-ended challenges in agriculture, arithmetic, civil government, classics, geography, grammar, Kansas history, penmanship, physiology, reading, spelling, and United States history. Many of the items had multiple parts. Typical of the agriculture section was a request for the student to name four plant diseases and how to control for each. Agriculture was included in country school curricula because many farmers believed that if it was studied, chances increased that the children could be kept "down on the farm." Testing in other areas was laden with rural imagery. A question in arithmetic might read, "If 15 hens lay 2 eggs each a day for 3 months when eggs sell for 12 cents a dozen, and 3 eggs a day for 45 days when eggs are 15 cents a dozen, how many dozen do the hens lay and what sum would the farmer realize?"

Other questions were quite philosophical. For example, students were asked in the civil government section to explain why government is necessary. In the classics, students were to give a brief biography of the author of the poem, "Evangeline" (Henry Wadsworth Longfellow). And in United States history, students were to give two reasons why every citizen should know history. Kansas students were asked to stretch their vision by responding to a question in geography about the cause of ocean currents.

On the other hand, many of the questions asked of students were quite practical. A question in the grammar section asked each eighth grader to write a 200-word letter to the clerk of their school board suggesting new equipment for the school. The Kansas history section asked students to write a paragraph on the growth of high schools in the state. The study of physiology in country schools was always related to hygiene, and thus the questions in this section emphasized the need for good health habits. Students were to contemplate why all drinking water should be pure, and whether or not alcohol possesses any of the three qualities to be classified as a food group.

Passing the eighth-grade exam was never a certainty; thus great joy was shared by the successful student and his or her entire family.

Country School Teachers

Among the noble souls who tried so hard to wipe out ignorance and illiteracy across the Plains was Howard Barnard. But was he a typical example of a country school teacher?

From Colonial times to the Civil War, most teachers in America were males. Even after the Civil War, as the Midwest was being settled, male teachers were preferred mainly because of their emphasis on strict discipline. However, as the Common School philosophy and ideas proclaimed by Horace Mann and Henry Barnard gained acceptance, more females were given a chance to teach. Common School educators believed that females, with their innate quality of motherly love, were more adept at imparting the Christian Nurture Doctrine than males. This doctrine held that God was a God of love, not one of anger and wrath, and that children were born without original sin and were not innately bad. Consequently, by 1900, women teachers were 70 percent of the work force. By 1930, in the rural schools of Kansas, women teachers totaled more than 90 percent of the work force. In addition to nurturing, women teachers had one other main advantage over their male counterparts — they worked more cheaply. In 1900, the average Kansas male teacher made $43 a month while a female was paid $36 — greater than a 15-percent pay difference. By 1930, teacher pay had changed very little. Not until the 1960s did Kansas school districts adopt single-salary schedules.

Most women country school teachers had rural roots. If they were one of the few who came from the city, it showed in many ways, not the least of which was when they tried to teach the required subject of agriculture.

Many had become teachers shortly after passing their county eighth-grade examination. Later, as high schools came into existence, students who had aspirations to teach could take a Normal curriculum during their senior year that prepared them to become teachers. Consequently, the beginning age for a country teacher was between 16 and 18 years old. As a result, students, especially males, were often older than the teacher because their education had been interrupted repeatedly by farm responsibilities.

For men, country school teaching was preliminary training for a later profession that might require work experience or even a college education. Teaching enabled them to save money to attend college. Some of the women did the same thing, although for others, teaching was what one did until marriage.

Assuming one had the correct attitude to teach and wished to do so, the country school teacher could attend two- to six-week summer workshops at Normal Institutes. Interestingly, these originally had been started by Howard Barnard's great-uncle Henry in Hartford, Connecticut, in 1839. His course consisted of lectures and field trips to actually observe teachers in action. Howard Barnard excelled at conducting these institutes on the High Plains. And in Kansas they were so highly regarded that the State Department of Education paid a county a subsidy of $50 if it could produce at least 50 prospective teachers for the institute. Like summer school on college campuses today, the mood, while for a serious purpose, was less formal and structured, and most participants looked forward to "hobnobbing" with like-minded educators. These early Normal Institutes were later called County Teacher Institutes, but their purpose never changed — it was to prepare participants to pass the county teacher examination.

The teacher exam was a two-day affair held in late June or early July, after the early summer teacher institutes were concluded. The subject areas were similar to the eighth-grade examination. However, as one may logically assume, teachers were tested over their ability to apply educational theory in the various subject areas. For example, in grammar, after asking several questions about why nouns have properties, the teacher-candidate was expected to outline a plan for developing a language lesson for the fifth grade. In orthography, teachers were asked to indicate where they would look for spelling lessons outside of school textbooks.

When considered collectively, social studies comprised the largest block of questions on the exam. In Kansas history, teachers had to know Kansas explorers, authors, prominent leaders, governors, acts of legislation, and finally what source materials they could recommend and use for children doing historical research on the state. In geography, they were asked to list ten imports of the United States and to draw a map of Kansas, locating major rivers, salt mines, sugar beet regions, and coal-producing areas, as well as the state colleges and penal institutions. In modern history, they were asked to explain the attitude of the monarchies of Europe toward the French Revolution. They were also asked how they would make use of newspapers in teaching world history. In civil government, they were to know the relationship of lawlessness in the classroom to poor citizenship in society, in general, and of family governance to state governance. In United States history, teachers were called upon to define terms such as initiative, referendum, recall, and short ballot. These could have been more appropriately included in the civil government section, but there was tremendous overlap of questions because each section was designed by different people, making the test a hodgepodge. In addition, they were asked to discuss the teaching of United States history in the grammar schools. Perhaps this would be a good task for most school boards to ask of their elementary principals and teachers today!

The absence of pure science questions shows an omission apparent in most elementary schools until the 1960s. The two areas closest to science were agriculture and physiology (hygiene). Teachers were expected to discuss the good and the bad effects of bacteria in the soil and to know and list the different types of wheat, as well as the daily food requirements for a working horse. In physiology, teachers were asked to explain how they would apply principles of hygiene in their schoolroom and to discuss fully the digestive work of the pancreatic juices.

In addition to an arithmetic section, there was a section on algebra. Teachers were asked such questions as "What should be the extent of first year's work in numbers?" They were also tested on arranging fractions in order of size. In algebra they were given five equations to solve and five story problems.

Four other areas were thoroughly covered: penmanship, music, reading, and teaching principles. The fewest questions were asked about penmanship, five compared to ten questions in all other areas. A typical question was "Which is more important in the first three grades, form or movement, and tell why?" The music section wanted to know if teachers could teach a two-part song and if they could find pitch for B-flat from a C played on a pitch pipe. In reading, they were asked to tell the relationship of imagination as a mental process to the process of oral reading. Additionally, they were to have written a course of study for the reading program in their school, prepared in advance of the examination. After all, reading was considered the most essential subject taught in the country school.

While many of the academic subject-area questions seem outdated, the questions on principles of teaching ring eternally true. Teachers were to have some familiarity with teacher certification. They were asked about the advantages of formally examining pupils. They needed to know something about the maturation levels of early childhood as opposed to adolescence and how teaching methods must be adjusted to meet the varying levels. Still, perhaps even more relevant today is the challenge: "How may teachers secure attention from pupils who are not interested in learning?"

A good educational psychology question was "On what does every mental image depend, and why is this important to teachers?" A corollary question was "Should vividness of imagination be cultivated or reproved, and why?" A philosophical question concerned the purpose of teaching. Teachers were asked to mention an objective of teaching besides imparting knowledge. Examinees were further asked to tell why it was good for them to attend teachers' meetings. Finally, they were to write an essay addressing the issue of rural school improvement.

Overall, this county-by-county, state-by-state teachers exam was as tough to pass and as hard to study for as today's National Teacher Examination that is a requirement for certification in many states.

For both men and women, an ultimate job in education might have been to become the county superintendent of schools. This position was an elected one, which was held by many women even before women had the privilege of voting. The county superintendent typically had the responsibility for a county's country schools, but no authority over city-run schools. The office of county superintendent, in place in Kansas for over 100 years, finally was abolished in 1967.

The state's early teachers signed contracts that rarely recorded anything except the school term (usually six to eight months) and the amount to be paid. Teachers were given a set of rules that more specifically outlined their duties, such as arriving early to start a fire in the stove. Men teachers could take one evening off each week for courting purposes; women teachers who married would be promptly dismissed; both sexes had to attend church regularly; money from the contracted salary was to be budgeted in order to save a portion for the "declining years." The rules were so thorough that they prescribed nearly every minute of the teacher's life during the contracted period. Much was expected, for farmers wanted teachers to be special role models for their young. In return, teachers were given great status and recognition in most rural communities. Howard Barnard was certainly no exception.

The Decline and Fall of Country Schools

If 1930 was the peak year for the one-room country schools in Kansas, which Howard Barnard had been so instrumental in improving and promoting during the later part of the 19th and early part of the 20th centuries, then he foresaw the movement toward consolidation and urban schools far ahead of others. With his Entre Nous School experiment in education in the first decade of the 20th century, he was at least 20 years ahead of his time. In fact, it would take Kansas another 60 years after the peak of country schools in 1930 to finally consolidate and leave behind forever the one-room public country school. It was in 1990 that the one-room Dermont School in far southwestern Kansas closed, the last of its kind. However, throughout the United States, there were still 430 one-room schools in existence in 1993.

Official criticism of rural school education began in 1896 at the national level as a result of a report by the Committee of Twelve, appointed by the National Education Association. This august body, composed mainly of school superintendents and college professors, consisted of three subcommittees appointed to study the state of rural education. Their combined reports found the country schools wanting, in the opinion of the 12 educational experts. They believed that the schools wasted money and that the instruction was inferior. At this time, bureaucracy, institutionalization, and high standards were goals of many professions and the American business community. Consequently, a "rural education problem" was targeted.

For the next 50 years, college presidents, newspapers, professional educators, and "city folk" would take up the crusade to abolish or reduce educational systems run by "country hicks." And Howard Barnard, because of his Eastern urban upbringing and Midwest country school teaching experience, was in an excellent position to lead the way to country school improvement without dismissing the ideas of his new-found friends on the farming frontier in Kansas.

Chapter 5

The Salvation of the Schools

We may not be able to raise wheat,
But we can educate our children.
Give them a long term and a good teacher.
Give the children a chance!
— Howard R. Barnard
July 4, 1902

Educational Concerns

*I*T is difficult for those living today to imagine the American schools of the 19th century. One important resource has changed — perhaps brainwashed — us forever, the development and implementation of the Stanford-Binet IQ Test at the beginning of the 20th century. Intelligence testing has given us some excellent insights into ministering to the needs of the children. It has allowed us to take better care of those who need special attention and reinforcement of learning. Such "special" education has been addressed in America like nowhere else on earth because of the utilization of this type of testing. One could easily contend that it has taken children out of the Dark Ages by aiding those who needed specialized education and giving them new understanding from their fellow students, as well as from their teachers and parents. That is the altruistic and positive accomplishment of this early 20th-century contribution to American schooling.

Unfortunately, there was a downside to IQ testing. It has also led to a type of linear thinking that is extremely fragmented. Parents and students tend to place children into such categories as "high IQ" or "low IQ" — or worse, "150" or "55" and thereafter limiting their perceived potential to achieve. The number representing IQ often delineates the type of material that is presented to a student — sometimes underestimating that individual's intellectual capacity. Teachers who should be aware of the limits as well as the diagnostic value of intelligence testing sometimes make these same categorical mistakes. One teacher could hardly wait to get the names of her new high school juniors, so that she could go to the school counselor and obtain each IQ score. Writing the score beside each name in the grade book before she had even seen the students subjected the students to prejudicial conclusions regarding their abilities.

The 19th century had an innocence about the equality of students' natural abilities that has since been lost. It was this simpler, more innocent, egalitarian, and perhaps even romantic concept of learning that formed Howard Barnard's concept of education. He believed that each of his students had been created equally and was endowed with certain rights, among them to receive a good education. For him this was measured not by some arbitrary score on an IQ test, but by that virtuous American quality known as "hard work," or as Barnard called it — effort. IQ tests have become to the 20th-century school what the work ethic was to the 19th-century school.

The Curriculum

It is evident that Barnard was influenced most by his great-uncle Henry Barnard. His work on the Kansas farming frontier was simply an extension of educational ideas that had been in the Barnard family for at least two generations. However, Barnard was also influenced by several others. At the top of that list was his uncle's favorite European educator, Johann Pestalozzi (1746-1827). It was Henry Barnard who had introduced Pestalozzianism to America in his book written in 1862 entitled *Pestalozzi and Pestalozzianism*. Pestalozzi was a famous Swiss educator who was influenced by both the romantic and the rational elements of the European Age of Enlightenment. Turning away from the ministry because he wrote poor sermons, and from a legal career because he feared he could not debate legal issues effectively before a judge and jury, he apparently decided to become a farmer because of his belief in the romantic nature of rural values. He had hoped to find a set of natural laws that governed learning, thus giving the world a "correct" set of rules for teaching and raising children. A few years after the birth of his only child, a son, Pestalozzi and his wife established a school for poor children on their farm at Neuhof, Switzerland. Although the school failed because of financial troubles, Pestalozzi established the model that would later make him one of the most respected educators in the world. Pestalozzi's school was based on the assumption that children are naturally active and that educators must capitalize on that activity by giving them exercises that foster vocational, moral, and intellectual development. In a sense, the children in a school act as an extended family, and the schoolmaster or schoolmarm should be like a father or mother rather than a pedantic principal.

Pestalozzi believed and proved that children could learn reading, writing, and arithmetic in the context of "worldly" work. On his farm, the children often recited lessons as they toiled in the fields, learning agricultural skills at the same time. Although Howard Barnard never went this far, he was a believer in combining the "real" world with the classroom. On more than one occasion, he dismissed his school children, loaded them in a wagon, and drove them to town for a political meeting. He stated that, after all, politics is a part of man's education, and it is well to hear all sides of a question and then choose the best. Barnard provided other field trips for his charges; he would never have been so one-sided as to allow only political experiences.

In Pestalozzi's best-selling novel, *Leonard and Gertrude* (1781), he outlined another concept that influenced Howard Barnard's thinking: the idea of home and school in concert as complementary stabilizing forces in the advancement of a child's education. Barnard subscribed to Pestalozzi's premise that this could best be done in a rural setting because that was the truly natural setting. Pestalozzi went so far as to suggest that these children, because they were able to develop their innate goodness in a loving, natural environment with emotionally secure adults, would turn out to be the leaders, capable of resisting evil and reforming the innate corruptness of society. Perhaps this concept was what had caused Barnard to exchange his life in New York City for the High Plains of Kansas.

Pestalozzi also believed in teaching by using objects that occurred naturally in the environment. Needless to say, this meant that one of the first lessons that all children had to learn was to respect all things in nature. From nature, all intellectual concepts were derived, broken into small components, and taught for total understanding. Children went outside and were shown a tree. They were asked to draw the tree, giving it form. Next, they counted the branches, giving them numbers. They would also be asked what the tree was called, giving emphasis to the sound. From form, number, and sound, children would go on to more complicated exercises that emphasized formal educational processes. Always, however, the method of learning began simply, with objects in the child's naturally occurring environment.

Howard Barnard embraced this concept of moving from the concrete to the abstract, from the simple exercise to the more complex, proceeding gradually and cumulatively. Barnard's regard for the environment was evidenced when he wrote to the *Western School Journal* relating the following, which was posted on his schoolhouse door:

> Let us not injure in any way any tree, shrub or lawn.
> Let us not kill or injure any bird or destroy its nest or eggs or young.
> Let us not spit upon the sidewalks or upon the floor of any schoolhouse.
> Let us not cut or mark in any way fences, poles, sidewalks or buildings.
> Let us always keep our backyards as clean and beautiful as we keep our front lawns.
> Let us at all times respect property of others as we would our own.

> Thus shall we become good and useful citizens, making our
> state beautiful and worthy of our love and devotion.

Barnard's basic beliefs about education and children were steeped in
Pestalozzianism. He believed in the innate goodness of all children, a
healthy respect for the environment, and the concept that all good teaching derived from the child's environment. While some of these ideas
were incorporated into the American Progressive School Movement of
the 20th century, and while Barnard certainly carried many of these
ideas into the 20th century in his years of teaching, for the most part,
these ideas passed into oblivion along with the 19th century.

Yet Barnard was too complex to be merely a naturalistic teacher. He
also believed, in the Jeffersonian tradition, that the purpose of education
was to prepare citizens to live in a democracy. He believed that to maintain a democracy, instruction was needed in a set of universally accepted
values, one of which was freedom.

Thomas Jefferson's philosophy of education, to which Barnard related, was set forth in Jefferson's Bill for the More General Diffusion of
Knowledge, which had been introduced in the Virginia Legislature in
1779. In it, Jefferson had left no doubt as to whom had fallen the responsibility to educate the young in a democracy. In his opinion, it was the
job of the state. Education was a civic concern for all people in a democratic society, not just the exclusive right of parents or the church.
Furthermore, every teacher had a responsibility to teach citizenship.
Barnard believed that the schools should not only teach patriotism, but
practicality as well. He honored Jefferson and the other founding fathers
by suggesting that a United States flag should be hung inside every
schoolhouse. He said that children would grow up to know the meaning
of our national emblem and to love and reverence the principles that
breathe out of its every fold. He predicted that in Kansas every schoolhouse would have a flag at an early date. Barnard also believed that education needed to prepare children with basic skills as a citizenship obligation. To him, good citizens worked hard at their jobs, just as elected
competent officials worked to serve their country. These basic attitudes
composed his curriculum.

Barnard's primary curriculum concern was how to get from his educational philosophy based on nature and citizenship to the real "nitty

gritty" of the 3Rs. But the task was made easier because Kansas and most other states had mandated a Common School curriculum by the turn of the century, based largely on the model and recommendations put forth by Barnard's great-uncle Henry when he had been educational commissioner of the states of Connecticut and Rhode Island. This Common School movement had started with the Pestalozzian idea of the natural child but was given an American religious twist known as the Christian Nurture Doctrine. Pestalozzi believed that children were born if not at least neutral, then probably mostly good. Therefore, if they were raised naturally, they would turn out to be good adults and citizens. In other words, the environment played the major role in shaping a child and not heredity. Pestalozzi believed that the curriculum must reflect this concept, that the overall aim of the curriculum should be conformity to the laws of nature and nature's God. An extension of this line of thinking would lead to the inclusion of citizenship preparation for all American children, including the inculcation of those skills that make a good worker.

Accordingly, Barnard's curriculum included more than the basic 3Rs. Barnard certainly believed in teaching the basics, but he would include much more. An examination of the talks that he gave to teachers at various meetings leads to the conclusion that Barnard felt there was nothing that could *not* be included in the country school curriculum.

Barnard believed, for example, that the teaching of singing and drawing was a step forward for the schools in the country. He was an early proponent for physical education and athletic programs for both boys and girls. He remarked that every university, college, and private school should have school-sponsored athletics, to include baseball, cricket, basketball, football, tennis, golf, horseshoes, and hockey. He questioned why the public school districts could not have their athletics well organized. He considered physical education to be just as important as moral, intellectual, or "book" learning. He thought it was an even third of a complete education, and sought to initiate such programs in his schools.

Barnard never did anything part way. One day, on February 2, 1900, he got so carried away with astronomy that he traveled into the town of McCracken and lectured the newspaper foreman about the relative position of the sun, moon, and stars. In a later educational column in the *McCracken Enterprise*, he explained the orbits and physical properties of the planets. Barnard taught the basics of reading, writing, and arithmetic, along with a healthy dose of science and history, art and music, and physical exercise. These subjects made up the formal curriculum, but there was a subtler emphasis that included instilling character-building traits that would make each child a good citizen and worker. To Barnard, the most important of these traits was self-reliance. He cited the following example:

> What makes the little newsboy on the streets so much sharper and wiser than the little patrician of his own age? Self-reliance. The little patrician has never learned to do things for himself. On the day of his birth he was turned over to a nurse who kept her eyes on him constantly, put him to bed, washed him, dressed him, and saw to it that he was neat and clean the livelong day. In time, the nurse turned him over to a governess, and she to a tutor. As soon as he went into knee breeches, he had a valet to dress him and take care of his wardrobe. If he had a little pain, his mother at once sent for a doctor and nurse. He was coddled and excused from his lessons. Whatever plaything he pleased to have, he got. When he wanted money, it came for the asking. He never had to think or do for himself.
>
> Quite different was the little newsboy's training. The son, possibly of a poor widow who went out washing and who had little time to watch him, had the sidewalks as his nursery and stern necessity as his tutor. He learned early to shift for himself. He had to fight or be kicked, so he fought. He had to hustle or go hungry, so he hustled. He had to dress himself or go naked, so he dressed himself. Often he had to patch his own clothes, cook his own meals, and make up his own bed.

According to Barnard, the contrast between the street boy and the rich man's child is greatest in boyhood. While the patrician lad is still confined to the back yard, the street boy is darting between the legs of horses, jumping on cars, peddling papers, and making his own living. Were it not for his superior academic education, the patrician would never be able to compete in the struggle for existence with the proletarian. School usually saves the rich man's son from being spoiled and ruined by his nurses and his mother. At school he finds the necessary competition and gets the necessary knocks and punchings that bring out his combative, self-preservative qualities and drill him in self-reliance. Howard Barnard considered self-reliance to be a necessary quality for honorable success.

> Until a man learns to do his own work, to fight his own way, to be his own patron and protector, he is worth nothing and will amount to nothing. Unhappy is the man who hangs on anybody's favor. It is shameful and degrading to need protection and to hide behind the shield of another person. The really successful man must stand on his own feet and go onward and upward by the force of his own character. The man who is not self-reliant is either a puppet or a parasite, and whether one or the other, he has a master.

Barnard perhaps pulled this parable from his own experience as a rich man's child in New York. It was ironic that he was envious of the poor newsboys whom he believed were not only streetwise, but also more self-reliant. Certainly, he wanted to instill this in his country school students, even by using urban examples (and maybe, *especially* by using urban examples).

Barnard also believed in teaching orderliness, promptness, and following instructions. However, his motives differed greatly from the captains of industry at the time who wanted schools to teach these things so that they would have an obedient work force. Barnard's intent was for his students to develop these traits for their own internal happiness. He said that self-improvement requires effort and that success requires strenuous, persistent effort. The greater the effort, the more rewarding the victory.

Barnard felt that it is only by hard work that we gain strength either of body or of mind. We should rejoice in those struggles that give us the sinews of our character. In the final analysis of life, each must stand on his own merit. He who has learned early in life to solve problems and conquer difficulties for himself, goes into the world with much greater strength than one who has always relied upon the aid of another. According to Barnard, education includes the ability to apply knowledge, and it is essential to success in any calling. A well-furnished intellect and a cultured will, Barnard instructed, are essential to happiness. The most powerful of all arguments for education or self-improvement is its beneficial effect upon the individual.

The Role of the Teacher

Howard Barnard believed that the teacher must make each pupil think. He cited Cicero, the Roman orator and educator, who said that man was born for thinking and acting and that it was incumbent upon each teacher to get pupils to think. Barnard admitted that some people think too little and talk too much; thus students should be taught the ability to strike a balance. He believed that he who thought the most did the most and that educators needed to teach students to do their own thinking. Thinkers, he believed, were admired. And because originality was more satisfying than just following along, students should be taught to think creatively. The best traveler sees things that others do not see, said Barnard; and the best thinker thinks things that others never dream of. Barnard related a parable to make his point:

> "Boy, what are you doing?" asked a teacher of the old school.
> "I am thinking."
> "Stop that at once! We don't allow any thinking here. Tell me what the book says!"

Barnard also had a strong belief that teachers should help pupils create proper learning habits. He believed, for example, that if pupils did not form proper reading habits by the fifth grade, the chances were great that they would never acquire good reading skills. Another role of the teacher was to show that labor is not disgraceful. Barnard thought that some people had little appreciation for the common laborer. But he believed that every job, vocation, or profession was equally respectable in America. He thought that each teacher had the responsibility of impressing this view on the students.

Another essential role of the teacher, according to Barnard, was to exemplify what he called supreme sympathy, teaching this by example, never fretting or worrying in front of the students. The teacher should be cheerful on a rainy day or on a "blue Monday." He believed, along with Emerson, that every day was the best day of the year — and with Browning, that no matter how many things go amiss, still "God's in his heaven — All's right with the world!"

Barnard also believed that social progress could be taught best by teachers showing good leadership because each school and classroom was a social institution in miniature. Therefore, the lessons learned at home and at church could be practiced in the school setting. If this was so, then the school was accountable to society at large, as was the teacher. Once the school had transformed social ideals and interests into habits, then it became an agency for social development, according to Barnard. The role of the teacher, however, was not to be that of a good babysitter or of the person who took children through their textbooks by recitation. It was to be a special calling to those who were most empathetic to the needs of childhood. A love of people, and the realization that children were people too, was a good starting point for a good teacher. Then, according to Barnard, some structure was necessary to organize lessons and keep students on track, thereby forming good work habits. Finally, a teacher needed to be morally a good role model for the children.

The "One Best Method"

Barnard believed that there was one superior way to instruct children and that it had special benefits for boys who, according to some educators, have had more trouble with formal learning than have girls. This instructional method was Barnard's own adaptation of the Pestalozzian "object" method, which began with what was known and worked toward the unknown. Barnard believed that the power to observe a simple thing and answer a plain question was the beginning of mental training. He firmly believed that if children were not instructed in this way, learning anything new would be much more difficult. Let the teacher, Barnard explained, ask the child to give an account of a well-known object such as an apple. The teacher might ask, "What is an apple?" Much time might be spent before any reasonable answer or description of an apple would be given. This teaching technique became what is known as inductive reasoning or "discovery learning." It takes time for the student to internally picture the apple and then to view it in many different ways, to compare it to other things similar to it, and finally to note how it is unique.

Barnard believed that by using this inductive process, any child could learn: the familiar object (the apple) was visualized; it was next contrasted with similar objects (oranges, pears, grapes); then its peculiarities, or differences, or uniqueness was noted (its color, its shape, its seeds, its texture).

Sight (the known) replaced thought (the unknown) as soon as a few plain instructions were given. To Barnard it was clear that the student could not possibly report on "nothingness" if the teacher started with a known object. He believed that all teachers should begin teaching with this Pestalozzian method. However, Barnard said that as teachers gained experience, other means would naturally occur to them that would work as well and would make learning skillful and effective. Barnard had great faith that his fellow teachers would discover their own ways of teaching, which might differ from his "one best method"; but they would not get an argument from him.

Barnard's major point about the methods of teaching was that children should be taught that learning is a science. If they acknowledged this, America would advance. Barnard further suggested that if the object method was followed, no teacher could come to the end of a term believing that the children had not gained from the lessons. He also believed that using this method alleviated discipline problems by keeping everyone involved in the learning process, thus connecting good teaching methods to efficient management procedures. According to Barnard, this type of teaching had another interesting result — it never occurred to children that the teacher was working. The students believed that *they* had done the hard work in the classroom, reaching the conclusions on their own, thus making them feel successful.

Barnard cautioned, however, that the teacher must always be alert for bad work, or rather, for students not working the right way. The process of learning, he said, was sometimes more important than the outcome. Every teacher must draw a strong distinction between faults of ignorance, which may be pardonable, and refusal to learn. Barnard had no patience with teachers who could not tell the difference. One can rest assured that he also had no sympathy for students who refused to be taught. He believed in individual responsibility.

Barnard's methods were quite "modern" for High Plains schools at the turn of the century. Some have been considered "progressive," as "new" waves of education reform hit the American scene every 30 years or so. Only the names of the methods change.

To understand Barnard's teaching strategy, one need only read a story that appeared in his "Under the Stars" newspaper column in the *McCracken Enterprise* on Friday, September 5, 1902.

The scene opens in the Prospect Street School of Cleveland, Ohio. The teacher was one of those drillmasters who wanted lessons recited just as the book gave them. He had no capacity to appreciate the genius of a 13-year-old girl who, though puny and timid, was quite sentimental in imagination. Matters of unrelated detail were difficult for her to grasp and added to her timidity. The drillmaster concluded that she was an idiot.

Enter upon the scene one Emerson White, at the beginning of his career as one of the most famous teachers in the country. The drillmaster told Mr. White that the pupils had been given numbers, were to read a problem, and should be called upon for the solution. Mr. White took the book, read out a problem, and called on student number eight. At this point, the drillmaster told Mr. White in disgust to call on another student because that one never could do anything.

Mr. White glanced along the row and at once identified student number eight, her sensitive, shrinking face drooping in an agony of shame and misery. Grasping the situation at once, White read the problem again, so that she was sure to understand it. Reading it slowly and clearly, he walked down the row and stood between the student and the drill master, the sight of whom he perceived filled the girl with confusion and terror. He assured her that she could do the problem, and to her own delighted astonishment, little number eight — who had never had the courage to speak a word aloud to the drillmaster — spoke up distinctly and went through the solution without a hitch. The child went home from school that day "perfectly transfigured," said her mother.

When the class was later divided, the girl was placed with Mr. White and went with him to the new Clinton Street School where she was a classmate of John D. Rockefeller, and A. L. Bartholomew, later a distinguished judge. All had been in the drillmaster's class together, yet he apparently had not discerned one ounce of ability in that entire group of children. In fact, student number eight had overheard the drillmaster indicating to Mr. White that there was not a scholar among the lot. This had enraged her, and she had turned to him in a blaze of indignation and cried: "How dare you say such a thing? We will be twenty percent ahead of your school in two years! Mark it!"

The gauntlet had been thrown at the drillmaster's feet, and the Clinton Street School of Cleveland was determined to make good the challenge. Perhaps they would have succeeded in any case, but they had the added fortune of having a born leader and organizer amongst them — Marcus Hanna.

Marcus did not content himself with learning his own lessons — that was no individual triumph. A class victory was needed, and that only could be accomplished by concerted effort on the part of everyone involved. For six months, by his arrangement and under his leadership, the class met outside of school to drill each other on their lessons and to strengthen their deficiencies. Emerson White did all that any teacher could to help and direct, but it was Marcus Hanna who kept the entire class at work. A prize would be awarded for drawing, so Marcus agreed with some of the students to go out early in the morning and sketch scenes from nature. As surely as morning came, there was Marcus under their several successive windows, throwing pebbles at the panes to awaken the young people. He organized a victory, just as he would later when he orchestrated the successful presidential campaign of fellow Ohioan, William McKinley.

Girl student number eight's challenge — "Mark it" — was recognized as a sort of class watchword. Of course, White's class won by the stipulated percentage.

Howard Barnard took kindly to this success story, as he viewed himself as the progressive, caring schoolmaster styled after one of his heroes, Emerson White. And he was.

The School Environment

Howard Barnard had some preconceived ideas about how schoolhouses should be constructed and furnished for the benefit of all students. He thought that every country schoolhouse should be built with the health, comfort, and intellectual and moral well-being of each student in mind. The building should be located in the middle of the grounds, on a high, well-drained plot, ornamented with trees and shrubs, and each school should have a well that supplied pure water. The architecture should be simple and should show a refined taste, because the schoolhouse itself was an educator.

Barnard believed that the schoolhouse should be built as well as the best home in the region so that children of well-to-do parents would not despise it and so that those of poor parents might see how the others lived and want to aspire to a higher level. Because to Barnard education was more than learning from books, the schoolhouse was to become an inspiration — almost a sanctuary — in the minds of the young.

Churches, Barnard said, were built as an example of noble architecture, to be an object lesson leading upward to a higher life. They should be grander than the houses of the worshippers, and yet the poorest man in the congregation should feel ownership as well. Furthermore, municipal and state buildings often display a community's ideal of a "home" for itself. And thus the schoolhouse should exhibit the taste and to some extent the aspirations of the neighborhood. It should be a little better than the best dwelling house in the country. The schoolhouse, as well as the teacher, should be a public benefactor.

With the dawning of the 20th century, with the excitement of the settlement of a new frontier, with the confidence that the people had faith in his progressive educational ideas, Howard Barnard, Yankee on the prairie, was ready for a new adventure. He would build his own school.

Chapter 6

Entre Nous College

Books, Schools, Education are the Scaffolding
By Means of Which
God Builds Up the Human Soul.
— Entre Nous College, 1911-1912 Graduation Souvenir

*I*N 1905, after teaching in schoolhouses in western Kansas for 15 years, Howard Barnard received an unexpected letter from New York. It informed him that he had been named as one of several heirs to a Barnard family estate. The administrator did not know the amount of the final settlement, and there was the possibility that it could be held up in the courts for several years. Nevertheless, Howard Barnard's wish was to be granted — he would have the means to build his own school.

For years, his dedication to bettering teaching practices on the frontier had brought enlightenment to members of his chosen profession.

Still, poor practices prevailed in rural America. Barnard believed in the dedication of these frontier teachers, but thought that their methods needed improvement — more than his summer institutes and training lectures at teachers' meetings could provide. They needed a model school! And now, with his inheritance, he would be able to provide one.

Barnard was boarding with the William Dourghty family at the time and was encouraged to pursue his dream by Mrs. Dourghty. One evening after supper, he put on his coat and hat and walked six miles to Abram Haas's neighboring home. He surprised Haas with his request to purchase ten acres of land upon which to build a school on a corner opposite the already existing Locust Grove School. Haas finally agreed to sell him four acres for $289 because his wife had fallen and injured her hip and he needed cash to pay the medical bills. Barnard was confident that if he took half a loaf, the other half would come, and eventually he secured the additional six acres for the ten-acre school site that he desired.

Before the end of 1905, Barnard had received $16,000, which made him one of the wealthiest men in the county. When word got around that he had come into an inheritance and was going to build a school, various school districts tried to persuade him to build it in their area. One of the most persistent districts was the Hillsdale School, which had the beginnings of a small town called Mills midway between the existing towns of McCracken and LaCrosse. But Barnard stayed with his original land purchase and his plan to build the school in the Locust Grove District. His perception of the people of the area was that they had a difficult time getting along with one another. Barnard was a true American idealist, believing that schooling would not only educate the children, but would unite the parents in a noble cause.

McCracken was also disappointed with Barnard's choice of Locust Grove. The McCracken newspaper editor stated that even though considerable lumber was being purchased from the lumberyard in his town for Barnard's new Locust Grove school, the building should be placed where it would not bar town scholars from attending. There were no boarding accommodations in the rural neighborhood and a ride of seven or eight miles for town children was impossible. The McCracken editor conceded, however, that Barnard's idea that city boys and girls already had every educational advantage possible was accurate and that rural

children had to put up with sometimes inferior teaching. And he com-
plimented Barnard by saying that wherever his school was located, it
would undoubtedly be of great benefit to students, based on the quality
of his past work.

As a result of Barnard's new-found wealth, and of his unique idea of
starting his own model rural school, people became more interested than
ever in this stranger who had been in their midst for the past 15 years.
Many of the more colorful stories about Barnard and his eccentricities
can be traced to this "school-building" phase of his life. It was at this
time that many people recognized the Barnard family as a force in the
American saga and, more particularly, in America's educational development.

Speculation first centered on where Barnard received his education.
Many believed, and passed on the story, that he was "Ivy League," educated at either Harvard or Yale. Barnard apparently did not discourage
such talk. But while it was true that his family had a long association
with Yale University, records indicate that he never matriculated there.
Nor did he attend Harvard or any other college. When pressed about the
issue, Barnard many times pulled out his Kansas Teaching Certificate,
which he always carried with him, and told the patron or reporter, or
whoever was inquiring, that it was the most important diploma anyone
could have. It certified that the great state of Kansas had placed infinite
faith in his ability to educate the children of the state. At that point, who
would argue with him? In fact, Barnard never attended a day of college
in his life. He never disclaimed a college education; he simply let people
believe what they wanted, pretending to be quite humble about his learning.

If Barnard's selection of a site for the school caused controversy, it
was nothing compared to his choice of who should build the school. He
chose a young man named Clarence Peer who was interested in becoming a teacher and who had attended several of his teachers' Normal
Training Institutes. However, Peer had very limited experience as a car-
penter or builder, and there were no drafted plans or blueprints. Barnard
told Peer that he wanted the school to be 30 x 40 feet with a 20x20-foot
hall and stairway, but he did not specify the height or the number of
rooms it was to have. He did tell Peer, however, that the building was to
be two stories.

Cost overruns and perhaps some shrewd practices by local business-men who had discovered that Barnard was not too practical about his labor of love ran his schoolhouse totals to more than $10,000. It should have cost half that amount.

Barnard did have the presence of mind to locate the school on the best road in the county. He decided against calling the school Barnard College, because one of his relatives, Frederich A. P. Barnard, president of the University of Mississippi and Columbia University, had already given his name to one of the first women's colleges in 1889. Barnard College remains affiliated with Columbia University in New York City. Since his days in 1902 as schoolmaster at the Star School, where he had students divided into two groups with secret names, Barnard had liked the name *Entre Nous*. Consequently, he used that name for his school. Some claim that he had never used the word "college," but "Entre Nous College" appeared on all of his stationery. Some patrons of the area mis-construed the name to be the French for "entrance free," rather than "among ourselves," and spread the word that Barnard was starting a pri-vate school that was to be free for all students. That was almost true, however, as Barnard charged only a minimal fee, $1.00 per month.

School Consolidation and Entre Nous

By the 20th century, it had become apparent in Kansas, and in many other states, that too many country schools had been built for the num-ber of students. Therefore, in 1901, the Kansas Legislature had begun to deal with the problem by allowing county superintendents of public instruction to combine schools with fewer than five students.

Barnard, always abreast of the latest educational happenings, had become an advocate for school consolidation, and his Entre Nous Col-lege would serve as a rural model by showing how to efficiently consol-idate several country schools, satisfying both students and parents. As early as 1902, Barnard had written that the interest and enthusiasm of pupils and teachers depended directly upon the number and ability of the pupils present. For the majority of children, he said, individual instruc-tion was not appropriate. Aristotle had condemned it on political grounds. Barnard believed that it was also bad pedagogy, that children needed the inspiration of numbers, which contain an ethical value. He thought that, as a rule, one could no more make a good school out of a

The Entre Nous College group photo with over 50 students. Note the lightning rods and the telephone pole. (Photo, Elva Paustian)

half-dozen pupils than he could make a powerful galvanic battery with one plate. Barnard also pointed out the cost effectiveness of larger schools stating that where pupils are scattered and the schools are small, education is necessarily very expensive, even if it is, at the same time, good.

To form the high school division of the Entre Nous School in September 1906, Barnard had consolidated the Hampton, Walnut Grove, and Locust Grove schools, the first successful such effort in the state of Kansas. He would later, in 1908, form his elementary division at Entre Nous with a consolidation of these same districts. In 1911, Kansas became the first state to pass legislation for comprehensive school consolidation. According to *Capper's Weekly*, a Topeka-based newspaper, the law was directly related to Barnard's successful experiment with Entre Nous School. Thus, Howard R. Barnard of western Kansas became the nation's "Father of School Consolidation."

This 1910 photo of Barnard's Entre Nous College, located east of McCracken on the Liebenthal Road, is the earliest remaining photo. It was taken by Cottage Studios of LaCrosse, Kansas. (Photo, Carolyn Thompson)

In front of the double doors with storm shutters, at the entrance of the Entre Nous School, was a framed garden area where Barnard planned to be buried. His grave, however, is at the LaCrosse Cemetery. (Photo, Shirley Higgins)

Unlike earlier such laws in other states, the 1911 Kansas School Consolidation Law set forth *how* districts could petition for school consolidation. They were to call for a meeting of the targeted districts and vote only after proper notice had been given. The decision would be made by a simple majority for or against. The process was to be overseen by the county superintendent of public instruction who also had the responsibility of holding meetings to create the new district should consolidation become a reality. At that meeting, a new school board consisting of a director, clerk, and treasurer were to be elected. Unfortunately, in Kansas and elsewhere, public funds were rarely available to enable people to consolidate in the high fashion that Barnard had with his Entre Nous School. Still, he had pioneered the new idea of consolidation as a positive advancement, not something negative, for the children of America.

By the 1930s, school districts in America peaked at over 130,000. By the year 2000, that number will have shrunk to under 15,000, an 850 percent decrease in 70 years.

The verdict is still out on whether students receive a better education in consolidated schools. When Nebraska tried to pass legislation in the early 1980s to consolidate its remaining 600 country schools, a legislative study showed higher college, law school, and medical school completion rates by former one-room school students than by others. The main reason for closing and consolidating country schools in Barnard's time, as well as now, remains financial.

Entre Nous Opens

When Entre Nous College opened its doors on April 16, 1906, it offered a Normal School training session for teachers of the area. The *McCracken Enterprise* reported that the building was not yet completed and was, therefore, not up to the standard expected. It also indicated that "Professor Barnard" had quite a few matters pertaining to the school that needed to be straightened out. Apparently, this was a reaction to an oversubscription of both teachers and students who wanted to attend the first session. It is noteworthy that Barnard felt that the training sessions needed students in order for the teachers to develop maximum competency. He believed that educational research concerned with methods and materials had to be tried and revised concurrently using actual pupils. Unfortunately, records do not indicate what new ventures in

The Entre Nous faculty in 1908-1909 consisted of three men and three women. Barnard is seated in the center, and it was thought that he was being nudged as a prank by Edith Miller.The faculty teased Barnard because he did not like to be touched. L to r: back row, John Crawford, George Walker, Principal J. T. Smith and his wife; seated l to r, Jean Swisher, Barnard, Edith Miller. (Photo, Shirley Higgins)

teaching Barnard had utilized during this first session, although he did indicate that a special emphasis was placed on the study of German and on music.

Barnard had hired two recent graduates of the Hays State Normal School as well as eight other professionals for this first course. However, the session was short, ending on Friday, May 11, with the notation that it could run longer if enough desired to attend. An exercise held on the last day consisted of a program and dinner, followed by numerous outdoor games including tennis, football, and basketball, which were played on the new grounds. This concluded the first Entre Nous College experiment in rural education. Teachers and scholars who had attended the celebration were joined by several families from the town of McCracken. Most educators must have gone away believing they had received their $2.00 worth from the month-long session.

It was fortunate that this first session did not extend for more than a month, because Barnard needed to finish construction and begin final preparations for the fall term, to begin with the high school division. He was very busy, as he was also becoming the most sought-after person in the county for all social affairs. He received invitations to most weddings, dances, and other galas. No one would forget to include him. And no one would forget to mention in the newspaper write-up that "Professor Barnard" was in attendance at their event. Because he loved people and loved the attention, Barnard was happy to oblige. He was especially pleased to witness the wedding of one of his favorite former students, Olive Landon, a beautiful, pleasant, and talented young woman who easily won admiration. After marriage to another native Kansan, Clarence Rogg, who had grown up a few miles away at Russell, the couple moved to Dayton, Washington. The marriages of Barnard's students became a frequent occurrence, and it seemed that many bright young people, once educated by Barnard and the other teachers, then moved out of the area to seek their livelihood.

By Thursday, June 7, 1906, Barnard had his Entre Nous schoolhouse in order. Leaving the sawdust on the floor, he sponsored a dance for the community. He sent 60 invitations and drew a good crowd. Once again Barnard was in the midst of Rush County social life. He may have been eccentric, but he enjoyed a good time.

Throughout the summer of 1906, Barnard sought out and hired what would become an exemplary staff for the start of the fall term at Entre Nous College.

The High School Division at Entre Nous

The American model for an educational system came from the English Sunday School: a superintendent, principal, and mostly female classroom teachers. From his classical 19th-century education and the influences of his great-uncle Henry Barnard, Howard Barnard knew of this system structure; and, since he possessed the pocketbook, he established himself as superintendent of Entre Nous College.

While contemporary colleges are associated primarily with students the age of high school graduates or older, that was not the case in 1906. "College" could mean any educational institution that attempted to instruct children — kindergarten through graduate school. Barnard chose to concentrate on elementary and high school. Therefore, Entre

Howard Barnard, surrounded by his upper division (high school) Entre Nous students, probably in 1911 or 1912. (Photo, McCracken Public Library, McCracken, KS)

Nous College had those two divisions. The elementary school was to include the typical grades one through eight. Kindergarten at the time was an urban endeavor and did not come to the western Kansas plains until the last half of the century. Barnard's high school division, the first of the two divisions to be opened at the Entre Nous School, was a novel idea. It was a rural classical high school with a four-year curriculum, which required a competent principal.

After considerable thought, Barnard hired Professor J. F. Smith, who had been the superintendent of schools of Stockton, Kansas, the previous year. Stockton was a thriving northwestern Kansas town, 60 miles north of McCracken. Smith had also recently presented himself as a prominent candidate for state superintendent of schools at the Republican Party state convention and was well known in state educational circles.

Smith had been born in 1863, in the first brick house in Kansas, a mansion belonging to The Reverend Thomas Johnson, a former long-

time superintendent of the Shawnee Methodist Mission and Manual
Labor School located in Kansas City. The building in which Smith was
born and two other permanent structures are preserved by the Kansas
State Historical Society and are listed as National Historical Landmarks.
Johnson County, Kansas, was named for Reverend Johnson, and the
school district in this Kansas City suburban area inherited its name from
this Methodist attempt at mission work among the Shawnee Indians.
Today the Shawnee Mission School District is one of America's wealth-
iest and finest school systems.

J. Franklin Smith was Howard Barnard's age, and being of the same
generation undoubtedly made it easier for them to work together. At the
time of Franklin Smith's appointment as principal of Entre Nous College, his father was still alive and living on the family farm in Linn
County that he had staked out in 1857. Smith's school life had begun in
Linn County in a one-room, log-cabin country school at the age of five.
His first teacher was Miss Mary Botkin, a relative of one of Kansas's
early Republican political leaders, J. T. Botkin. He spent his early school
days learning to speak English, because German was spoken in his
home.

At the age of 20, J. Franklin Smith had enrolled at Baker University,
located in Baldwin, Kansas, just a few miles southwest of Kansas City.
He studied there for six years, graduating in 1889. It was at college that
he met Susie Knight, a local girl from Baldwin and a Baker University
graduate. On May 29, 1889, shortly after his graduation, they were married. The following year, they left to seek their fortune in what was to
become, for a time, the capital of Oklahoma, Guthrie. Smith engaged in
real estate and studied law. He was also an active participant in the newly
formed Republican Party and became friends with many Oklahoma
politicians.

In the summer of 1891, Smith became president of Cumberland
College in Greenfield, Missouri. At 28 years of age, he was one of the
youngest college presidents in the country. His wife occupied the Chair
of Latin and German Studies at Cumberland, thus starting a joint effort
that continued throughout their entire lives. But they held these first
educational positions for only two years, before land fever got into
their blood. They left for Guthrie in 1893, just before the Cherokee Strip
Run.

Ironically, this was the same run that had intrigued Barnard, but Smith was more successful than Barnard had been, as he had secured some excellent land in Newkirk, Oklahoma. While in this Indian Territory, Smith once again became an educator. He organized school systems in three cities, Lexington, Pawnee, and Pond Creek, and he gained a reputation as an educational innovator by his advocacy for a graded school system, placing each grade through the eighth in a separate room. This was quite a departure from the one-room country schools where all grades were together.

In 1896, the Smiths returned to eastern Kansas where J. Franklin took the job of principal of the Williamsburg schools in Franklin County, southwest of Ottawa. However, their stay in Kansas was short-lived, as a year later, Smith once again was asked to become president of Cumberland College. After mulling over the appointment, the Smiths decided instead to matriculate at the Kansas Normal School in Emporia, Kansas. In 1898, both J. Franklin and Susie Smith graduated from the Latin program. During the next seven years, the Smiths held a variety of educational posts in both Kansas and Missouri. J. Franklin was the principal of schools in Dorrance, Quenemo, Hartford, and Ashland, Kansas. Susie held at least one teaching job at a college in Merwin, Missouri.

According to letters of recommendation to Barnard, the Smiths were excellent educators. In one dated June 30, 1904, President J. N. Moore of Interstate College, in Merwin, Missouri, stated that Susie Smith was the strongest and most popular teacher among the faculty. Mr. E. H. Murlin, president of Baker University, at Baldwin, Kansas, was equally complimentary of Franklin. He wrote that Franklin was an energetic, reliable, and worthy man of confidence and esteem. Perhaps the best and most telling letter for both Smiths came from Mattie Wallingford-Baker, the county superintendent of schools in Ashland, Kansas. She wrote that J. Franklin Smith was thoroughly competent as a teacher and principal, and that he had solved various difficult problems of school governance for the system and was a strong disciplinarian. She also stated that Susie Smith was very capable in the management of her classes and that her ability was beyond question. She went on to suggest that the Smiths were leaving their current educational posts to go to Entre Nous College because they desired and deserved more money. Ashland or Stockton, or any other small Kansas country school system, could not possibly compete. Obviously, Barnard chose the best faculty for Entre Nous College that money could buy!

It did not hinder matters that the Smiths several years before their 1906 Entre Nous appointments had purchased a wheat farm of 640 acres near McCracken where they enjoyed spending summer vacations. Barnard hired both Smiths at double their previous salary. It was Barnard's plan to do this with all of his faculty members, making them the highest paid in the state. He believed that one of the faults of rural education was that teachers were poorly paid and that for that reason, they continued to be of poor quality. Barnard's logic was simple. Well-paid teachers would have increased self-esteem. That would make them feel better as people and they would then be better as teachers. Their increased morale would be passed along to the parents and students. Barnard justified the high salaries by saying that if his teachers were not worth more money, then they were not worth having! At its zenith, Entre Nous College employed a faculty of six, a janitor, and several "kid-wagon" (transportation) drivers.

Barnard firmly believed that the reason children initially left the farms of western Kansas was to attend high schools in the newly emerging cities. His creation of Entre Nous College and its high school program was an attempt to solve this problem. He also believed that a high school program could offer the rural community the much-needed cultural and recreational facility that no one-room country school could hope to provide. He knew that there was a tendency for rural children to end their education after eighth grade. The fact that the world was rapidly changing would put children with only an eighth-grade education at a considerable disadvantage in the future.

While Barnard may be termed a progressive educator, he was conservative when it came to the school's curriculum. He believed that the classics would best prepare students for the larger world. Consequently, there are few surprises in the Entre Nous high school curriculum. During the first year, each student studied Latin, algebra, English, and physiology. The second year continued the first-year basics with Caesar (in Latin, of course), ancient Western history, English with emphasis on rhetoric and composition, classical literature, and plane geometry. In the third or junior year, each student took Cicero (also in Latin), complete algebra, English literature including Shakespeare, and medieval and modern world history. In the senior year, students deliberated Virgil (in Latin), physics, economics, zoology, American history, rhetoric, and the United States Constitution.

There is a great similarity between Barnard's curriculum and what became known as the college preparatory track in American public high schools by the 1920s. But Barnard believed strongly that this was not simply a curriculum for the college-bound students. If it helped them get into college, fine and dandy! But he believed that this curriculum would make students totally functional, intelligent, and articulate adults. This was preparation for life, and every student should experience it. Barnard later expanded his high school curriculum to include agriculture, book-keeping, commercial arithmetic, and physical education.

When the doors of the Entre Nous high school division were formally opened on September 3, 1906, only one student, the Smith's daughter, Grace, attended. However, the Smiths educated her well, albeit rather expensively for Barnard — Susie Smith's salary was $1,200 for the year. The division of teaching duties allowed Susie Smith to teach Latin and all other languages, while Frank Smith covered math and science, as well as history. For the next year, Barnard expanded the curriculum, hoping to attract more students. His persistence paid off, and the second year saw three students enroll in the high school division. The third year there were five. One, John Crawford, was also the janitor. However, the only person to graduate from the high school division was Grace Smith.

And what did Barnard do in 1906? He was independently wealthy and could have chosen to rest on his laurels as superintendent of Entre Nous College. Instead, he continued to teach in a one-room country school, Locust Grove, across the road from Entre Nous, while he completed his plans for the opening of the Entre Nous elementary division. He was paid $25 a month for eight months of teaching at Locust Grove. He was also elected president of the Rush County Teachers Association. And as he had done for so many years before, he continued to present lectures at the teachers' meetings. The year 1906 saw him emphasize the essentials of physiology and hygiene.

When the spring of 1907 broke forth, Barnard was eager to hold the second teachers' institute in his new building — so eager that he expanded the term to six weeks for the same $2.00 fee, and charged half that amount for students under 17. The term began May 1, 1907, and continued until the middle of June, ending just before the busy western Kansas wheat harvest. Because six weeks was a long time for some of the participants to be away from home, Barnard had a telephone installed. This was most likely the first telephone in a rural school in the state.

Barnard was still not ready to start the elementary division of Entre Nous School in the fall of 1907, so he taught at Hampton School for that term. He continued to preside over the Rush County teachers and became rather "pushy" about attendance at meetings. He pointed out that it was not only their duty to uplift themselves, but that if they held professional certificates, they were required by the state of Kansas to attend. Barnard was probably interpreting the law somewhat liberally to suit his own needs, but he said that he was prepared to print the names of all teachers attending in order for each school board to identify those who took their jobs seriously. The meetings were all-day affairs and were always held at Entre Nous College.

The Elementary Division at Entre Nous

Barnard finally managed to open the elementary division of Entre Nous School in September 1908. The building itself was adequate to accommodate both divisions on the first floor. An auditorium and a library were on the second floor. Because he had persuaded the parents of the three districts to consolidate with his college, the Locust Grove School, which was across the road, was vacant. It thus became the location for the primary division (grades 1, 2, 3) of his elementary classes. Barnard believed that this saved the tiny youngsters from being teased or tormented by the older children. Also, they were not as likely to be hit by baseballs on the playground.

Barnard's elementary division followed the state curriculum and was similar to the one that he had used in his one-room country school teaching. However, he insisted that Entre Nous would follow the Revised Course for City Schools circulated by the State of Kansas Department of Education, as it was much more challenging than the one for country schools. He attempted to establish a graded elementary, by dividing the students into the primary grades (1, 2, 3) with one teacher and the upper elementary (4, 5, 6) with another. Because the principal of Entre Nous, J. Franklin Smith, was something of an expert on graded elementary

The Entre Nous third and fourth grades. Next to Barnard, the most remembered teacher at Entre Nous College was a lower grades teacher, Edith Miller, pictured here with her students. (Photo, Carolyn Thompson)

Jean Swisher's Entre Nous fifth and sixth grade class consisted of mostly boys in 1908-1909. (Photo, Carolyn Thompson)

schools, the experiment, the first of its kind in the area, was considered a success.

School began at nine o'clock sharp with a worship period. If students came early, they entered the building to begin studying quietly. Barnard would push a button in his office that rang a bell in every room. The primary division would march (not walk) over to the college building, go upstairs through the high school division, and enter the auditorium. The students passed Superintendent Barnard as they entered the auditorium for a kind of inspection. He sat, leaning back with one finger on his cheek. Pupils came to learn that when he was angry, the top of his bald head became red and his eyes bore a hole right through them. Once all students were seated, there was a prayer, Bible verses were read by a student, and hymns were sung. Barnard's favorite, "Higher Ground," was heard every day. At the conclusion of the hour-long service, the students marched back to their classrooms.

In their respective classes, there were several noticeable changes from the country school agenda. First, each student recited standing by his seat, rather than taking an embarrassing trip to the front of the classroom, sitting on the recitation bench for what seemed like an eternity, and waiting for a line of students in front of him. This was perhaps a small innovation, but huge in terms of the psychological facilitation of learning. Barnard also had every student keep a separate notebook or journal for each subject studied. He believed that this would help them to better understand what they were studying. Students were encouraged to work out their thoughts in detail and to write complete explanations about what they observed. For example, in math, after a problem was worked, students wrote down how they had worked it and gave the reasons for each step of the solution. Barnard was a perfectionist when it came to penmanship, and the entries in each journal had to be more than merely legible to satisfy him.

Barnard placed great emphasis on the classics at the secondary level and on the basics for the elementary. He believed that the basics were the gateway to the classics and ultimately to intelligence as an adult. Barnard also placed priority on music and physical education. His interest in music was influenced by both his great-uncle Henry Barnard and the famous educator Horace Mann. They both believed that music unified students and was a method of teaching self-discipline as well.

This is the Entre Nous high school division of 1908-1909, with the faculty seated. (Photo, Carolyn Thompson)

Barnard considered music aesthetically pleasing and thought that it gave rural students some exposure to culture. In his school, students participated in singing at the worship services, as well as studying music in their classes. Music was introduced as an activity, not simply a passive listening experience, although that was included as well.

Barnard employed George Walker, a former Army officer, to be a full-time physical education teacher and athletic director. This appointment was controversial because most professional educators and community citizens alike could not see the rationale of hiring a teacher who did nothing more than teach children to play games. Barnard thought differently. He had Walker teach the children the discipline of marching, as well as all manner of playground games, to insure that each student exercised and participated in some gaming activity each day. Walker also began school athletic teams that competed with teams from the community.

Barnard also continued his field trips, which he had initiated in his country school teaching. The *McCracken Enterprise* of March 27, 1908, records that Professor Barnard and his scholars had paid a social visit to the McCracken Grade School the previous Wednesday and that the visit was much appreciated.

By 1912, Barnard's elementary division had enrolled over 100 students. They were taught by Edith Miller, Jean Swisher, and Grace Copeland, in addition to George Walker and Barnard himself. Little is known about any of their whereabouts following the close of the Entre Nous School.

Entre Nous Contributions

While the school consolidation concept might be considered Barnard's greatest educational contribution, there were at least six other innovations to his credit. One of the most significant was his "kid wagons."

One chilly winter morning as Barnard watched the younger students straggle into the school with their feet wet and cold from walking as far as five miles, he conceived the idea of transporting the children himself. He was the first educator in Kansas to develop the notion that it might be the responsibility of the school to get children to their early-morning destination as a courtesy to parents. So Barnard purchased an enclosed wooden farm wagon and converted it to a "school bus" of sorts. The wagon was drawn by a team of two horses, so for their own safety the children entered from the rear. There were seats around the inside wall, and plenty of lap robes to keep their small bodies warm. The greatest luxury of all was the foot warmers, which insured total comfort. There was a curtain between the driver and the young people. Imagine being one of the privileged students of Entre Nous College riding to school in such comfort while fellow students in rural areas all across America were hiking two to five miles daily through cold, rain, and snow. Barnard was the "Father of Busing" in Kansas, if not throughout America.

The kid wagon created quite a stir in western Kansas. Public schools could not match Barnard's transportation plan. When one wagon was not enough, he purchased two more. Barnard paid rent to three area farmers for overnight storage of the wagons and for feeding the horses in their barns, and he constructed a shed to protect the wagons and horses once at school. Three routes began each day from the farmers' homes, and children were picked up along the way to the school. The longest route was nine miles.

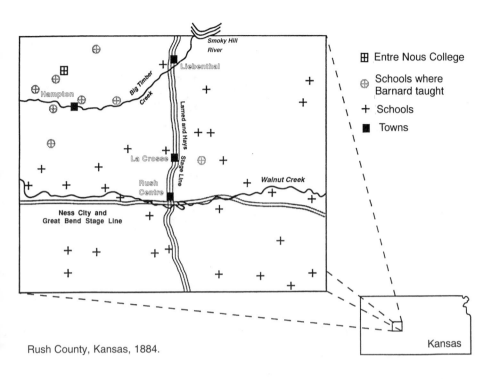

Rush County, Kansas, 1884.

Barnard, always the advocate for strong bodies as well as minds, created a magnificent playground at the Entre Nous School, where tennis, baseball, basketball, and track could be enjoyed by girls as well as boys. (Photo, McCracken Public Library, McCracken, KS)

By today's standards, Barnard's Entre Nous College grandstand leaves much to be desired. By standards for schools at the turn of the century, a covered grandstand like this was a luxury. The girls in the photo are playing basketball. (Photo, Barnard Library, LaCrosse, KS)

One of Barnard's innovative practices was to run bus routes (three of them) with the converted farm buggies that he called kid wagons. Here they are pictured in front of his Entre Nous College. (Photo, Shirley Higgins)

Even though Barnard never rode a horse during his cowherding days, he commanded one of the teams of horses and drove one of the wagons each day. The other two drivers were two of the older Entre Nous College students. Of course, the farmer Barnard lived with, Frank Start, had to hitch the horses for him every morning, and frequently, Start had to rush Barnard along to prevent him from being tardy. One of Barnard's favorite delays in driving a kid wagon was taking his student passengers far out of the way to see a new baby that had been born in the community. He so believed in the beauty of the beginning of life that he wanted all of his charges to share in the experience. He also wanted to bring his personal congratulations to the new parents.

For all the miles that the kid wagons rolled, there was only one serious accident. In December 1910, a student, Mamie Nelson, was thrown out of the back of one of the wagons. An automobile had frightened the team of horses, which, in turn, had reared up. Nelson was knocked unconscious, but she recovered in a few days.

A classic rural curriculum was an obsession of Barnard's for the high

Entre Nous baseball stars, George Ree, and Bud and Bill Foster played on the school's boys baseball team. Note the E.N.C. on Bud Foster's jersey. (Photo, Printcraft Printers, Hays, KS)

school students, but where did he get his idea for agriculture as a necessity for all students? Most probably, there were two sources. The state of Kansas required all students to have some knowledge of agriculture, as they were tested over it on the state-wide examinations for an eighth-grade diploma. Also, at about this time, the Hays Normal School had decided that its main emphasis would be teacher training in agriculture. They hired a professor, Josiah Main, who influenced Barnard to teach even the elementary school students about agriculture.

At Hays, students had plots of land for gardens in which they planted a variety of vegetables in order to conduct experiments — radishes, lettuce, onions, spinach, beets, peas, and beans. Barnard provided the same for his Entre Nous students. He set aside a full acre for after-school agricultural experimentation. Students were learning firsthand about agriculture and possibly were passing along information to their parents before there was such a thing as a county farm agent. Some of the farm families were skeptical of this agricultural experimentation and perceived it as a "fad" perpetuated by those well-meaning, but highly theoretical, professors at the Hays Normal School. However, this skepticism paled in comparison to the criticism he received for his physical education program.

That program, designed by Barnard and his physical education director, George Walker, resembled the Prussian education model of emphasis on conditioning the body as well as the mind. Walker had instituted a physical exercise program that included calisthenics, marching, and athletic competition. Gradually, however, the community came to accept this rather unusual program because they were included in it. On the Friday following the Thursday Commencement Exercises in May, the Entre Nous Field Day was held. An invitation was extended to the entire community to come out to Entre Nous College and participate in an all-day competition of games and activities. The morning exercises for youth under 16 consisted of potato, egg, bean, barrel, and sack races. The program in the afternoon included baseball, basketball, jumping, and tennis matches. Girls from the athletic association provided lunch and lemonade, which points out something else unusual about the physical education program at Entre Nous. It was for both boys and girls. Entre Nous had competitive athletic teams in basketball, baseball, and tennis for both sexes.

The first field day at Entre Nous, on May 15, 1908, was the largest event ever held in Rush County to that time. The editor of the *McCracken Enterprise* estimated that there were over 600 people in attendance. It was a gala day and one to be remembered and repeated. The editor suggested that the McCracken Band reeled off one great number after the other, apparently all in key!

The following term, the success of the Entre Nous College physical education program showed in its athletic teams' endeavors. The boys baseball team of 1908, which included a pitcher named Claude Stephens who had perfect control, speed, and a vicious curve ball, went undefeated. The Entre Nous College girls basketball team also had a perfect winning record against the LaCrosse girls, although they had just enough players for one team and could not afford to have anyone foul out.

In 1909, an expanded field day saw additional races for youth: relays, and hoop, pie, shoe, and obstacle races. The program accommodated both young and old, large and small. There were also more field events such as pole vaulting and hammer throwing. Track events included a half-mile run for boys and men, as well as hurdles, and a 50-yard race for girls. Some novelty games included nail-driving contests for girls and women, an over-25 tug of war for men, a baseball throw for women, and a Siamese race. But 1909 brought a new problem — automobiles. They had to park on the Locust Grove School grounds across the road from the college. The women of the Nickel Cemetery conducted the coffee, lemonade, and lunch stand, and the Entre Nous College boys held an ice cream social.

In 1910, the field day grew even larger. Included was a greased pig chase for men over 18, and each event had a prize. A mechanical merry-go-round was set up by Barnett's Amusement. Its music box rang out its solitary tune for miles around.

Throughout the year, Entre Nous College held numerous track meets on its grounds with teams from the region competing, including teams from the Hays Normal School. Usually, Entre Nous put on a play, such as *Jedediah Jackson Judkins*, or some other cultural activity as a culminating event on the evening of the track meet. By 1910, educators throughout Rush County, Kansas, were aware of the benefits of physical education and were incorporating Barnard's and Walker's ideas into their own curricula. The Rush County Teachers Association even included athletic programs on several of their literary program agendas.

Another contribution of Barnard's Entre Nous College was its physical facilities. Although he was not an architect, Barnard had gleaned from his prior teaching experience what children needed, and he laid out the school yard accordingly. He had baseball and football fields complete with bleachers that would hold 300 spectators. An outdoor basketball court and a lawn tennis court, as well as a large all-purpose playground, were north of the building. He considered the natural drainage of the land, as well as it accessibility to the roads. Cement sidewalks connected the main points on the grounds with the southern entrance to the main building. Barnard knew that his building needed large windows to allow natural sunlight for students to write and read. He ordered real slate for blackboards, which was something of a novelty in the West — extremely delicate and difficult to transport, and very expensive.

The interior walls of the Entre Nous School were light green in color, in accordance with the thinking of the time that green stimulated creativity. Barnard's school was the first in the area to install a central hot-air furnace, fueled by coal. He also purchased adjustable seats and desks that were complete units in themselves. The school had indoor plumbing and running water, as well as imported gas lamps and the telephone. Each of these additions was a first for the region. Barnard was providing a model for rural education that did not take second to city schools.

A nicely appointed auditorium on the second floor of the building had dressing rooms and a grand piano that were better than any auditorium in any of the small cities of the county. And when Barnard had implemented his kid wagons, he had also built the wagon barn not only for his three wagons and six horses, but for as many as 20 horses of students who could ride their own animals to school. The barn loft doubled as hay storage and a gymnasium.

Continually doing something unknowingly controversial, Barnard proposed making Entre Nous College a free and open community center. But citizens were curious about his position that although the college was open to all social, religious, and political groups, they could not discuss their creeds or sectarian differences either from the stage of the auditorium or over the newly installed telephone. Also, there were to be no insulting remarks made by anyone that would slander another person.

This barn, located on the Entre Nous College campus, housed the three kid wagons and the six horses that pulled them. (Photo, Carolyn Thompson)

Two groups that managed to overcome their doubts about the school's open-door policy and use Entre Nous College as a meeting place were the Sunday School Convention and the Republican Party in 1908. The churches of McCracken dismissed their usual Sunday worship services to allow members to attend the Sunday School Convention on April 26. Barnard, a non-churchgoing sort, even participated as a presenter for the intermediate grades. The day-long events concluded with a basket dinner and singing, undoubtedly in the auditorium using the grand piano. Barnard many times served as a consultant to the churches for Sunday School material that he would order for them from a large variety of publishing houses.

If Barnard was not a Republican, he was a close sympathizer. He hired mostly people with a Republican bent, supported Republican candidates, and never once held a political meeting at Entre Nous other than Republican. It is entirely possible that no other political organization ever asked him for the use of his facility. Nonetheless, the Republican Party chose to end its Rush County campaign on Monday, November 2, 1908, before election day, at Entre Nous College. Republicans were encouraged to come early and stay late to give the candidates a big reception. Ladies were encouraged to attend this political affair. There was to be good speaking along party lines, plenty of music, and a general good time. Barnard provided a phonograph machine on which were played several speeches by William H. Taft, the Republican presidential nominee, who subsequently won the election.

Eventually, people of the community frequently used Entre Nous College for parties of all kinds, and it was booked months ahead for Christmas and other holiday affairs. Barnard particularly liked the annual Thanksgiving Eve Oyster Stew Party, as it took him back to his New England roots. Entre Nous was truly a community gathering place!

But the most amazing contribution of all at Entre Nous was the library. Although most country school libraries contained fewer than 100 books, Barnard had managed to purchase and collect over 3,000 volumes. His Entre Nous library was larger than some college libraries and probably was the largest high school library in Kansas. Books were Barnard's obsession. He was always buying books and thought more of them, according to many of those who knew him, than he did of himself. Several stories bear this out.

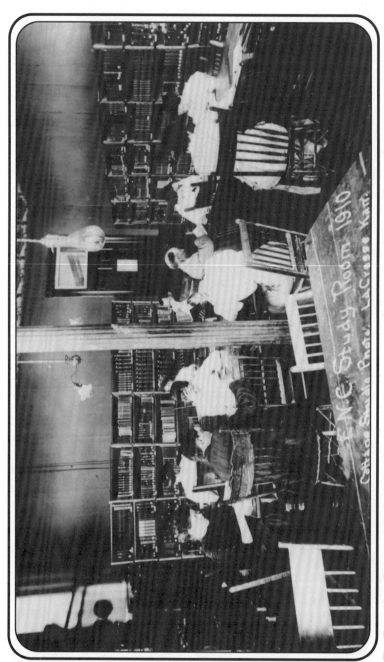

The Entre Nous College study room. By 1910, Barnard's library was called the study room; it was well supplied with long tables, comfortable chairs, and electric lights. (Photo, Barnard Library, LaCrosse, KS)

As superintendent of his school, he continued what he had done many times as a teacher. He would leave the Entre Nous College grounds around 4:00 p.m. and head northeast cross-country to pick up the Fort Hays-Fort Dodge Trail. He would walk 25 miles to Hays to Robert Markwell's Bookstore. Markwell often opened his store for Barnard late at night, so that Barnard could shop. Barnard would make his purchase, then return to Entre Nous before dawn. Even with snow covering the ground, he sometimes walked the distance in the dead of winter. He wore a heavy corduroy suit, and when he tired of walking, he wrapped his suit coat around him tightly; then with the collar up and the ear flaps of his hat down, he would lay in the snow until rested. On one occasion when rain fell, he took off his coat, wrapped it around a borrowed Fort Hays Normal book, and got soaked to the bone.

In 1910, Barnard began making the first of many lectures about the importance of the school library. He gave the first talk to the Rush County Teachers Association on Saturday, February 19. They held their annual spring institute in LaCrosse in May of 1911, and Barnard conducted the study room, as he had done previously. That year, his hauling of five wagonloads of the Entre Nous library books to LaCrosse did not go unnoticed. The newspaper proclaimed that the teachers attending had an advantage over many large colleges because of his library. Many of the teachers appreciated Barnard's library so much that they asked to borrow his books during the school year. When the institute was over, after some thought, he employed Clarence Peer, the builder of his school, to construct 40 strong shipping boxes. In these crates, Barnard sent books to teachers all over the western part of Kansas and eastern Colorado — not yet an interlibrary loan system, but close!

School finance has always been a major problem in both public and private attempts to educate America's youth, with the exception of some fortunate universities. A saying of Barnard's time was "money oils the machinery and makes it run good." Entre Nous was no exception. It received all of its "oil," except for the $1.00 per month charged each student's parents, from Barnard's inheritance. A guardian appointed to oversee the estate had allowed him to spend only the interest on the principal. In 1912, he received a letter noting that the estate was being contested and that he would receive no more money for the present, perhaps not ever. In typical fashion for him, Barnard did not legally pursue the

A rare photo of a "beardless" Howard Barnard at the Entre Nous library with his prized books. (Photo, Printcraft Printers, Hays, KS)

The stove that Barnard purchased for the children in the elementary division of Entre Nous College is housed in the Barnard Library, LaCrosse, Kansas. (Photo, Allan Miller)

matter, but rather accepted what the letter said. He eventually mortgaged the school building to continue to pay salaries and expenses.

On August 10, 1913, *The Kansas City Star* newspaper ran an article entitled "A Short Grass Light That Failed." Rather than attempt to explain it locally, the *McCracken Enterprise* chose to re-run *The Star's* article in its entirety on August 15. Unfortunately, the article was correct — the 1912-1913 sessions at Entre Nous College were to be its last. These two sessions were teacher institutes that Barnard taught himself because he could no longer pay his staff salaries. He resided in the building at the time and lived like a pauper. His diet consisted mainly of beans and potatoes, cooked on a small children's stove intended for use by the elementary students enrolled there. (This stove can be seen in the Barnard Library at LaCrosse, Kansas.) People frequently saw him walking along a road with a cold potato in one hand and a salt shaker in the other. Barnard's diet was supplemented occasionally when a thoughtful farm wife would send him some homemade bread and a glass of jelly.

Barnard had foreseen financial trouble as early as August 1911, when he had procured a loan for $298 from the McCracken Citizens State Bank at ten percent interest. Then, in 1912, the Waterman-Waterbury Company of Minnesota sent Barnard a bill for $312 for a stove they had installed. It was to be the final payment, but he did not have the money. So he borrowed it from the Farmers and Merchants State Bank of LaCrosse at six percent interest. But Waterman-Waterbury never received the check, and they brought suit against Barnard, as he had listed Entre Nous College as collateral. On April 21, 1912, Barnard once again got the money to pay the Waterman-Waterbury loan by signing a promissory note to James E. Rice of the McCracken Citizens State Bank for $400 at ten percent interest. On December 14, 1912, Barnard was sued by Rice for the $400. W. H. and Frank Russell were the attorneys for the plaintiff.

A proof of publication was printed for four consecutive weeks in February and March 1913 in the *LaCrosse Republican* newspaper and signed by Leonard Young, Clerk of the Rush County Court. On March 29, 1913, Barnard's Entre Nous College property that had been used as collateral against all three loans was sold by the Rush County Sheriff, J. M. Russell, from the steps of the courthouse. Waterman-Waterbury, the original plaintiff, purchased the property for $1,214.40. The attorney fee paid to W. H. Russell, brother of the sheriff, was $1,165.25. Barnard had invested over $40,000 in his noble educational experiment, and after subtracting attorney's fees, Entre Nous actually was sold for $49.15. The land later sold for $1,500 to Oscar Elias.

One can speculate on other reasons why the college failed. In a personal interview with Barnard on November 26, 1937, he told Darlienne Thompson that he had overspent on the stove and that had really put him under. He also suggested that the backwardness of Rush County in the fight to locate the county seat had caused many hard feelings. Consequently, newcomers found other counties in which to settle and raise their children. Others have suggested that Barnard's school would have been more successful had he located it closer to the center of Rush County, rather than so near the Ellis County line. But late in life, Barnard admitted that he was a poor manager of money. Entre Nous, the Short Grass Light that failed, was proof.

Chapter 7

Books and Basics

Never mind whereabouts your work is,
Never mind whether your name is associated with it.
You may never see the issue of your toils.
You are working for eternity.
If you cannot see results in the hot working day,
The cool evening hours are drawing near
When you may rest from your labors.
And then they will follow you.
                              — Howard Barnard (1902)

BY the end of 1914, the remnants of Entre Nous College were gone. Barnard's creditors had stripped the prairie of the beautiful two-story, white-framed building by tearing it down for the lumber. Around 1918, even the kid-wagon barn was hauled off by several teams of horses. The materials from Entre Nous built at least two houses in the town of McCracken. The land, purchased by Oscar Elias, was plowed under and planted in wheat. Today, the corner of the Entre Nous plot has been returned to native prairie buffalo grass and has a Kansas post-rock limestone monument commemorating Barnard's "object lesson." When the monument was originally built in 1975, the large Entre Nous school bell was cemented into the top with bronze plaques denoting the site of the school. The Oscar Elias family donated the bell and the small plot of land for the memorial, and the McCracken Community Club and the Health and Home Unit were responsible for erecting the remembrance. Like so many things in American culture, the memorial has been vandalized, and it is missing two of the three bronze plaques. Still, on the wind-swept plains of western Kansas, it serves as a reminder of the innovative educational experiment of Entre Nous and simpler, more traditional times.

In 1913, Howard Barnard started his career anew at the age of 49. The ghost of Entre Nous College and its failure would weigh heavily on him for the rest of his life; he considered its failure his own personal failure. However, Barnard chose to bear the burden; and although the buildings of his noble experiment were taken from the High Plains of Kansas, he remained! He was a tremendously honorable person, promising to stay in Rush County and work until all of his debts were totally repaid. He was Yankee to the bone!

In 1912, Barnard had entered into a verbal contract with the McCracken School Board to move his library of over 3,000 volumes to town to be used by the pupils of the public schools. A room was to be "fitted up" for the purpose, and Professor Barnard was to have complete charge. The library was to be accessible to anyone who desired to use it, but a newspaper item noted that his books were especially adapted to students. The move to McCracken did not materialize, and the books stayed in the Entre Nous building until May 1913 when Barnard moved them to the basement of the First Christian Church in LaCrosse. He did this in anticipation of the annual Rush County Normal Institute that he had been helping with for years. The church basement was equipped better than any of his previous "Normal study rooms" because Barnard had hauled *all* of his books from Entre Nous to the LaCrosse Institute rather than only the ones he believed to be most pertinent to the teachers. Decorated attractively, the church basement had an inviting appearance

Thirty-two horses were used to haul away the Entre Nous kid wagon barn after it was sold. (Photo, Shirley Higgins)

Ralph Plotner is shown here at the Entre Nous College Memorial with its bell set in concrete on top at the site of Barnard's "noble experiment." Plotner attended and later taught at Entre Nous College. The bell and land were donated by the Oscar Elias family. Two service clubs from McCracken oversaw the project in 1975. (Photo, Barnard Library, LaCrosse, KS)

and seemed to be a place where they could be safe and used. But strangely, at the conclusion of the institute, Barnard hauled his books back to the Entre Nous School, which was by that time, in the summer of 1913, being used as a private residence. Barnard, however, was extended the courtesy of storing his library there.

Barnard was a genuine educator at heart, and thus it was not surprising that he returned to teaching in a country school. Nor was it surprising that the country school he chose to assist in was once again the Hampton School. One day in the fall of 1913 while teaching there, Barnard received a letter from H. L. Baker, one of the LaCrosse city fathers, asking him to consider bringing his library permanently to the town for use as a city library. In return, he would become the city librarian. Perhaps to help persuade Barnard, Baker convinced the editor of the *LaCrosse Republican* newspaper to place a notice on the front page of his paper on November 13, 1913. It suggested that the city could get a library of 7,000 volumes (his estimate was considerably exaggerated, as Barnard had only 3,000) for free. He asked readers to imagine stacks of books running 71 feet in cases as high as a man could reach. He said that the collection was worth over $2,000, and that a librarian could be secured for 67 cents a day (presumably Barnard). Opportunity was knocking! To guarantee that his plea would be read, the editor placed this front-page notice as an extension of another short notice with the headline "Found Insane."

Ironically, as Barnard was reading his letter from Baker, the clatter of a motorcycle outside the school caught his attention. When he went to the door, he recognized Charles Bitters, principal of LaCrosse High School. Bitters had ridden out to Hampton School to talk to Barnard about an alternative library proposal. He asked Barnard if he had received the letter from Baker, and Barnard acknowledged that he was, in fact, just reading it. Bitters persuaded Barnard to donate his library instead to LaCrosse High School and to become its librarian beginning that December.

Barnard accepted Bitters's offer for two reasons. First, and foremost, Barnard would be able to continue his work around young people. In addition, he considered the LaCrosse High School building a safer building, particularly from fire, for his 3,000 volumes. If he had accepted the city's offer from Baker, his library would have been housed in a frame building on Main Street. He thoughtfully considered the fact that if he or the city had to buy fire insurance, that meant less funds for books. Also of interest to Barnard was the promise of a new high school building housing a library complete with a central lavatory. It would be equipped with soap and nail brushes where students could wash their hands before handling Barnard's books.

On December 1, 1913, Barnard's books became the major part of the LaCrosse High School library, located temporarily in the north study hall room of the elementary school building. At first, the books were placed on shelves around the outside of the room, because the library also served as an assembly hall. Barnard's beginning salary as LaCrosse High School librarian was $60 per month.

The *LaCrosse Republican* considered the development nothing short of a coup by the LaCrosse School Board. The paper was especially impressed with Barnard as librarian, stating that he was a wonderful student of literature in his own right. According to the newspaper, the LaCrosse High School students had a better chance of obtaining a complete education than any other students in Kansas because of Barnard and his reference books. The editor even said he believed that LaCrosse High School was nearing perfection as a result of this move. With renewed vigor because of the faith placed in him as a librarian at LaCrosse, Barnard became a loyal booster of his new town, its schools, its students, and especially its library.

By January 1914, Barnard had the library books neatly shelved and ready for the people of the community as well as the school children. A notice placed in the newspaper stated that the public could check out books during school hours as long as they promised to abide by the library rules. Barnard, who was referred to as Professor Barnard, extended the hours of the library for the public in March 1914. He kept it open Saturday and Sunday afternoons from 1 until 5 o'clock. He was not only generous with his books, but also with his time.

Barnard continued to use his own salary to buy books and subscribe to newspapers and journals. But he also expected the school administrators to have the same enthusiasm for purchasing books that he did. Unfortunately, he found out in fairly short order that this was not the case. As one supporter of Barnard put it, the superintendent was not on a mental par with him.

Although Barnard was financially destitute except for his monthly salary, in October of 1914, he made a trip to Entre Nous College and hauled a load of school desks back to LaCrosse to help relieve the overcrowded elementary classrooms there. Quite possibly he could have sold the desks to help settle his debts, but the comfort of children in their classrooms took precedence in his charitable decision.

By 1916, the nearly 3,000 volumes in the LaCrosse High School library were moved by the 80 high school students from the combined grade-high school into the newly completed, fireproof, high school building. At the time of the move, the *LaCrosse Republican* reported that only seven high schools in the state had larger libraries, and that all were in larger city schools in the eastern part of the state. The promise made to Barnard that his books would be housed in a new brick structure with the latest library design had been kept. But Barnard did not foresee that he would not accompany his books into the new high school building, the most modern high school in the western half of Kansas at the time. Barnard was fiercely independent and had little patience with the superintendent, George L. McClenny, who would not purchase books. Barnard was also in conflict with the administration over library rules. While Barnard was loved by most of the students, he was strict and quite orderly where books were concerned. The superintendent thought his rules were overbearing and, in the winter of 1916, he fired Barnard from the librarian's post.

Once again without a job, and still heavily in debt from Entre Nous, Barnard spent the remainder of the winter living in the LaCrosse railroad depot. Many of the town women had grown fond of Barnard, who represented to them the highest form of culture in their new city. They vehemently believed that he had been wronged by the superintendent. In 1912, the women of Kansas had received the right to vote. Many were just beginning to believe that they could play an important role in civic decisions. It is no coincidence that the women of LaCrosse decided to exercise their relatively new civic responsibility by taking up the cultural cause of the library. What is more important, they took up the cause of the librarian, whom they believed had been ill-treated by what they perceived as an anti-intellectual school superintendent.

On November 19, 1916, women of the community held a public meeting in the Rush County Courthouse, which produced a new organization called the Barnard Library Association. It collected donations to meet Barnard's sparse living expenses and was able to get him reinstated as the high school librarian. The school administration agreed to tolerate Barnard's presence as long as the library association paid his salary. The association also became the purchasing agent for acquiring new books. It held "book showers" that yielded many volumes. Admission charged to certain meetings of the association was a book, and all were contributed to the Barnard collection in the high school library, which was rapidly becoming a community library.

In the fall of 1917, Barnard returned to teaching at Hampton School. He received a regular salary of $55 per month for the seven-month term. However, he struck a deal with the LaCrosse school district and the library association to leave all of his books in the high school. He insisted that any book that belonged to him be labeled "Hampton School" and checked out under a separate system.

But his particular and demanding ways had disastrous consequences. The complex and convoluted check-out system he had required unknowingly gave students an open challenge to take his books. So many of them disappeared that he personally removed the rest to a private residence in the country that to this day remains a secret. Barnard accused the LaCrosse high school administration of perpetuating this theft.

The beginning of the 1918 fall school term found Barnard teaching in the South Fairview-Benbow School, four miles east of Hampton, for the same salary and seven-month term as he had the previous year at Hampton. In the fall of 1919, he changed to yet another Rush County country school, Brown School. In 1920, Barnard began what would be a four-year teaching position at a Quaker school located in the Friends Meeting House near Hargrave, Kansas, a small town between McCracken and LaCrosse. At this point in his career, Barnard was once again secure enough to unpack his books and keep them in the Friends school.

Although the Barnard Library Association had formally disbanded, the thoughts of the members were still with Barnard and his magnificent love of books. And he did not harm his cause any by presenting papers and leading discussions on "The Value of a Library to a Community." Between 1913 and 1923, he presented no fewer than 21 formal programs on the topic in both LaCrosse and McCracken.

At the annual LaCrosse school meeting in 1923, high school parents and patrons gave the board of education a mandate to bring back Howard Barnard and his books. They wanted him reinstated as the LaCrosse High School librarian. Barnard was pleased. With his consent in the fall of 1924, his books and those of the high school were once again combined and housed in the LaCrosse High School building.

Also housed in the LaCrosse High School library were books belonging to the newly re-established Barnard Library Association. This group was an outgrowth of an idea put forth by the Delphian Club, one of LaCrosse's better social and reading clubs for women. It enlisted the aid of three other women's study clubs in LaCrosse to establish a board of directors made up of officers from the four clubs. Other clubs wanted to be included and were gladly welcomed into the fold. Gradually, 11 clubs became involved in sponsoring the Barnard Library Association: the Delphian Club, Review Club, Monday Evening Club, Sunflower Club, Conomore Club, Business and Professional Women's Club, American Legion Auxiliary, Auxiliary to the Veterans of Foreign Wars, Daughters of the American Revolution, Women's Christian Temperance Union, and Crescent Club. Each club had two representatives on the board of directors, each representative serving only one year, so that a large number of LaCrosse women served and became ardent supporters of this celebrated organization. To these early pioneer women, the library was too important to the community to be left in the hands of the school board and the school administration. The Barnard Library Association and the school board worked out arrangements whereby anyone living in the LaCrosse High School district could use the books. In at least one early 20th-century town, LaCrosse, Kansas, the library and its books were jointly owned and operated by the public schools and the women of the community. From the early days of the American frontier, promoting culture seemed to be an almost exclusive domain of women.

In December 1926, the Barnard Library Association received a charter from the state of Kansas making the high school library the official library for the city of LaCrosse; fundraising entertainment and membership subscriptions supported it. Although many believe that private business/public school partnerships began during the Ronald Reagan presidency with its emphasis on private enterprise in the 1980s, in 1926, on the western plains of Kansas, a perfect, much earlier, example defies that perception. Barnard did, however, receive his salary this time from the public school system.

Howard Barnard, as LaCrosse High School and city librarian, had finally established and was firmly entrenched in his new occupation, thanks to the fortitude of the founding mothers of LaCrosse. Barnard's decision at age 49 served him well for the rest of his life. By the middle of America's roaring '20s, Barnard was no longer a transplanted Yankee on the prairie; he was a Kansan!

Higher Ground

Lead me to the Rock that is higher than I. . . .
— Psalm 61:2

Johnson Oatman, Jr.

HIGHER GROUND
Charles H. Gabriel

1 I'm press-ing on the up-ward way, New heights I'm gain - ing ev - ery
2 My heart has no de-sire to stay Where doubts a - rise and fears dis -
3 I want to live a-bove the world, Though Sa-tan's darts at me are
4 I want to scale the ut-most height And catch a gleam of glo - ry

1 day; Still pray-ing as I'm on - ward bound, "Lord, plant my
2 may; Though some may dwell where these a - bound, My prayer, my
3 hurled; For faith has caught the joy - ful sound, The song of
4 bright; But still I'll pray, 'til heaven I've found "Lord, lead me

1 feet on high - er ground."
2 aim is high - er ground.
3 saints on high - er ground.
4 on to high - er ground."

Lord, lift me up and let me stand By faith on heav - en's ta - ble - land, A high - er plane than I have found: Lord, plant my feet on high - er ground.

"Higher Ground" was Howard Barnard's favorite hymn. It was sung every morning at Entre Nous to officially open each school day. (Photo, *Baptist Hymnal*, Convention Press, Nashville, TN)

Chapter 8

The Librarian

Books are keys to wisdom's treasure
Books are gates to lands of pleasure
Books are paths that upward lead
Books are friends. Come, let's read.
— Howard Barnard, 1927

$\mathcal{S}$OME contend that on the Great Plains, anything worth doing takes twice as long and encounters twice the number of problems. Howard Barnard must have felt this way about establishing a library. It had taken him ten years to accomplish his goal, and it had not been an easy chore for Barnard or for the community. In 1924, his library was a reality only because of the persistence of the ladies of LaCrosse and their ability to function as a powerful pressure group that eventually persuaded Barnard to return to their community. Once he had made that decision, he was so excited about it that he announced that

he would open the library for the summer even though his contract as
high school and city librarian took effect in September.

Barnard's library had a unique atmosphere that captured the attention
of the students and patrons as soon as they entered. He was fond of mottos and slogans and displayed them long before it became fashionable to
do so. One of his favorites, a line from the hymn "Higher Ground," had
been written on a cardboard cross and suspended from his library ceiling:

> I'm pressing on the upward way; new heights I'm gaining
> every day. . . .

The words were visible as soon as anyone passed through the main
entrance. Where Barnard found others of his mottos was unknown. But
on one occasion, he gleaned one from a morning chapel talk. He thought
the words "Do not dodge difficulties; meet them, greet them, beat them"
were so good that they should be adopted as the school motto for the
year, and he had them printed on pink cards for each student and faculty member to carry.

Barnard was fascinated with anything that might improve education.
It was no surprise that in the center of his library was a new electric pencil sharpener, which kept shavings off the floor — a novelty to students
in 1925. Over 15 years later, Barnard would still surprise students and
patrons with new gadgets, including Rush County's first public drinking
fountain — a Frigidaire — that kept water cool using electricity.

What patrons of the library in LaCrosse remembered best, however,
was not the facility but rather the man. He was short and bald with pierc-
ing blue eyes and a full white beard. He nearly always wore a white shirt
and suit trousers held up by suspenders. He rarely engaged in conversation, and when he did, it was with a noticeable stammer. His gentle
appearance made him an unlikely leader of the library and enforcer of
his strict rules. Nonetheless, most respected him because they knew that
everything he did ensured respect for books and the knowledge they
contained. He made his library a sanctuary from all outside interference.

Early in his career as librarian, Barnard had developed the idea of
printing the rules of his library on small pieces of paper for individual
distribution to each patron. At first, these rules were simple and straight-

Howard Barnard became the premier rural librarian in Kansas. Here he sits at his desk with his "summer cut" beard. Note the photo of him on the top shelf. (Photo, Elva Paustian)

forward. Later, however, the original two printed pages was expanded to eight pages. His early rules had stated the hours of operation, which remained constant throughout Barnard's career. As long as the library was connected with the high school, the library was open from 8:00 a.m. until 12:00 p.m. and 1:00 p.m. to 5:00 p.m., then 7:00 p.m. to 10:00 p.m., Monday through Friday. If someone needed to stay later than 10:00 p.m., Barnard always obliged. To him, knowledge didn't necessarily end at a certain time; knowledge was not time bound.

The most frustrating rule in Barnard's library was that requiring total silence, a rule relentlessly enforced. Barnard thought that there were no exceptions because no one had the right to disturb another, who might be gaining wisdom. If someone was talking or whispering too loudly, Barnard would blow his infamous whispering horn in their face. This manual air horn was similar to an old-fashioned bicycle horn. Such a practice would not get a librarian or teacher very far today, although Pat Conroy in his book, *The Water is Wide*, reported inheriting such a whispering horn in a poor all-black grade school in South Carolina in the 1960s. He used it as a positive reinforcer for students who gave correct answers.

A corollary rule to the silence requisite, however, showed some flexibility about talking in the library — a minor miracle considering Barnard's strictness. The rule stated that communication corrupts good manners — get permission first. Even in Barnard's library, one could talk, albeit very quietly, if one received permission.

Barnard's rules also required that all chairs be placed under a table upon "rising." In addition, no one was to use ink in the library to copy library material; it could spill too easily and ruin a book, or it might be used by not-so-clever students to write in the covers of books. To reinforce this, Barnard made a poster of a large tiger sleeping, with a small monkey just about ready to grab the tiger by the tail. The motto read:

Never twist the tiger's tail or use ink in copying from library material.

The "no-ink" rule led directly to a positive — or at least instructional — rule: bring a notebook and pencil. Barnard acknowledged that his patrons might find something to copy from his books, especially the encyclopedias. And, as an attempt at adding a little humor to his rules, Barnard purposely misspelled and combined the first three words of a sentence thusly.

> Uneeda pencil of your own while doing business in the library.

One might conclude correctly that anyone who would install lavatories in the middle of the library would also have a rule regarding clean hands. Barnard insisted that care should be taken at all times to have clean hands when handling and reading all library material. He expected careful usage and also expected that any damage to the books would have to be "made good."

Barnard's rules for check-outs and fines conformed to those of other Kansas libraries. The books could be taken out for seven days, with the possibility of renewing for another seven. For books kept overtime, a fine of two cents a day was imposed.

The rule that Barnard was most noted for, however, was his rule for using the dictionary or "old Dick" as he called it. With both hands, one was to place the dictionary on its back with fingers of the right hand over the back cover and fingers of the left hand over the front cover. The right or left thumb, as the case may be, was to be placed on the black letter required. In this position the book was to be opened. To close "old Dick," one was to lift both covers at the same time. Students were instructed to write out their lists of words in alphabetical order before using the dictionary. A final dictionary and book rule was to turn all pages from the upper right hand "dry fingered."

Former student Elva Paustion remembered that she was frightened by Barnard when checking a book out or returning it. He had a certain way that all books were to be placed in a paper bag and tied with a certain kind of twine when being transported. Each student or patron was taught how to do this and was expected to comply. Upon return of the books, Barnard would inspect the paper package to see if the book had been wrapped properly. If it did not pass his inspection, he would give another lesson in the art of wrapping books and how to tie a square knot to hold the brown paper bag around the book.

As time passed, because the library added additional services for patrons, Barnard added more rules. But he never gave up his original set. They may have seemed old fashioned to some by the Dust Bowl days of the 1930s, but they gave Barnard a good grip on the helm of his ship. The rules worked, and therefore they would not change. To many of the 1930s teenage students in LaCrosse, this inflexibility made Barnard appear eccentric and hard-nosed.

Prior to the beginning of World War II, Barnard had believed in the idea of the perfect Kansas high school library. He and other Kansas school librarians thought that each high school class should be housed in a separate room from the study hall. Although the library should be well supervised, Barnard did not believe that it was the librarian's main task to manage students in a study hall. That disciplinary task remained for others. Barnard thought that these high school libraries should all be equipped with tables, chairs, shelves, a loan desk, magazine racks, bulletin boards, and a catalog case. The library should be large enough to accommodate from one-tenth to one-fourth of the total high school enrollment.

Barnard also had some thoughts about the organization and control of the high school library. He believed that it should serve every department of the school. He thought that all libraries must be card indexed and catalogued, using the Dewey decimal system. He stated that this card system should be constantly updated and revised, otherwise it would be of absolutely no value to anyone. Books that became ragged and unsightly needed to be mended, replaced, or discarded. And the order of all libraries should be "quiet," as this was the best atmosphere for study.

As far as books were concerned, Barnard thought that each library should have a set of approved encyclopedias, dictionaries, and atlases. A formula was one modern encyclopedia for every 50 students. Barnard believed that every Kansas high school library should have ten books for every student enrolled. Periodicals and newspapers must be provided to meet the requirements of the course of study for the school. At least one good periodical should be provided for each department in the high school, with ten being the minimum for any school. He suggested that each library subscribe on a service basis to *Reader's Guide to Periodical Literature.*

It was the job of every librarian, according to Barnard, to instruct each

"Don't Flinch. Don't Foul. Hit the Line Hard"

B²

LIBRARY LAWS

OF THE

RURAL HIGH SCHOOL

AT

LA CROSSE, KANSAS

COMPLIMENTS OF

H. R. BARNARD

LIBRARIAN

Howard Barnard was honest with students, and to help them be the same, he passed out complimentary booklets — "Be Square" — paid for by himself, of the library laws. (Courtesy, Barnard Library, LaCrosse, KS) pupil in the use of the library. This could be done individually or in groups or classes of students. But, it must be done by the librarian!

How did the librarians find appropriate books to purchase for the library? Barnard said that all books for high school students should come from one of two sources: either the Kansas State List of Books, put out by the Department of Education, or the American Library Association's *Books for High Schools.*

Barnard also had some thoughts on the library's physical environment. Of course, the library must be well lighted, and it must also have a sanitary drinking fountain. The heating and ventilation system should supply a sufficient quantity of pure, fresh air, heated to a uniform temperature of 67 to 70 degrees.

Not only did Barnard conform to all of the standards he advocated, he exceeded them considerably. Barnard had over 25 volumes per student in his LaCrosse High School Library. And by the end of the 1930s, he subscribed to close to 100 magazines and newspapers, most of which he paid for out of his own pocket.

Barnard devised a system of traffic signal lights, which were placed outside the library entrance door. A green light indicated to the patron that there were vacant chairs in the library; a red light indicated that the library's chairs were full, although one could still come in.

In the 1930s, Barnard began his "library laws" booklet, which he freely distributed, with a message intended for teachers as much as for students. He said that anyone could see that society was changing and that it was nowhere more evident than in the field of education. School had become less of a teaching factory and more of an environment. The teacher's role in the enterprise was to furnish the environment with stimulants to get students to respond. He saw the library as the laboratory of the school. He said that the modern high school was built totally around the library. He observed that one need only recall the day of the single textbook in contrast to the method of the modern 1930s where the teacher would lead a class in problem-solving by consulting all available information and opinions on a subject with the help of the library. Unfortunately, too many teachers in the late 20th century do not understand what Barnard meant.

Barnard's position as LaCrosse librarian during the 1920s, '30s, and '40s, was due in part to the reorganization and revival of the Barnard

Library Association in April 1925. This time, seven women's clubs of the city established a library board that worked closely with the high school board of education. One of their first acts was to allow anyone living in the entire rural high school district to check out books. Previously, check-out privileges were limited to students of the high school and members of the association. The newly reorganized association reported that the library contained 3,000 books that belonged to Howard Barnard, nearly 400 books that belonged to the high school, and 125 books that were credited to the city library, which was the association.

An announcement in the newspaper suggested that Barnard should be consulted about the selection of stories appropriate to one's interest and reading level, as well as for reference work one might need to do. In another article, the paper noted that LaCrosse had the distinctive feature of having the best library in western Kansas, as well as that rare oddity, a paid librarian. Strangely, whenever the salaries of other public employees were listed in the newspaper, Barnard's name appeared in the list, but the amount he was being paid was absent. It is likely that he requested that the editor omit his salary. It *was* a simpler time!

Barnard was said to be of inestimable value to the children of the community mainly because he seemed to have about as much information in his head as did the books in his library. In June 1925, the newspaper proclaimed Barnard the best librarian in the state of Kansas. It was suggested that a good way to improve one's mind was to visit him at the library.

By 1926 the reorganized library board was able to purchase 76 new books with money from its private library fund. The books were ordered in January and received in April. By that time, enough new money had been added to the fund to order another shipment of books. The board was quick to notice that several of the new books were mistreated by patrons. They notified Barnard that he was to charge a patron the cost of the book if it was returned mutilated. The board stated that the rule was put in place not because of financial considerations, but because it wanted books treated with respect.

The library board also decided that the selection of new fiction could best be handled by a "pay shelf." A charge of five cents per book was to be made for the check-out privilege from this shelf. The money would go into a separate account specifically for the purchase of additional fiction. To buy the other books for the library, the LaCrosse Harmony Orchestra offered to give a benefit concert in May 1926. It was directed by LaCrosse photographer Ardin W. Conard, whose avocation was music. His father was a band leader, and Ardin later purchased a Garden City radio station. The concert gained $65 for the library (using Department of Labor's Consumer Price Index, $584 in 1994 dollars). At the same time, it was announced that LaCrosse was the only city in its classification in the entire state of Kansas to have a paid librarian. LaCrosse citizens were justifiably proud.

So proud was LaCrosse of its library that the opening statement in the local newspaper advertising the high school for the fall of 1926 proclaimed that LaCrosse had one advantage over all other high schools in the state — The Barnard Library and Professor Barnard himself. Barnard was in top form. He prepared short reviews of some of the new book arrivals for the newspaper, which came under the curious title "Station B.L.A. Broadcasting." The B.L.A. undoubtedly stood for Barnard Library Association. This was his attempt to keep current and be clever, as radio was catching on across the country.

Barnard reported in 1926 that students used the library far more than adults. Surely Barnard knew that such would always be the case with a library attached to the high school; but this apparently was another gimmick to get the parents and other citizens into the library — make them ashamed that their children were showing them up, and adult business for his library might increase.

During 1927, library benefits continued to bring in much-needed money for books. The first, held on February 14, Valentine's Day, was a concert called "Girls in Song." Twelve girls of the community dressed in foreign costumes presented solos, duets, and quartets. Names of the twelve were withheld so that the audience could try to guess their identities. A party was held after the concert in the high school gym, and people paid in proportion to what they ate. This benefit netted $119.

Two new ideas apparently popped into Barnard's head concerning the library at this time. Parents had told him that he was so successful with getting small children to read that they had no way of knowing what or how many books their own youngsters were checking out. Barnard thus decided that each child should have a note from one parent stating permission to check out a book, though he hoped that this rule would not inhibit the children's enthusiasm.

He also decided to have a special Library Day on June 21, an open house to get acquainted with the library. From two until three o'clock, he planned something "especial" for all children old enough to read. From three until five o'clock, all older folks were invited. Tours were given and light refreshments were served.

Eighty-four patrons — old and young attended the Library Day. Barnard had everything in readiness. Small plants were given to everyone. Children were entertained with stories told by Winnifred Russell, the high school music director, and then were allowed to look for books that interested them. On their tour of the library, the adults learned that 80 percent of all libraries in the United States were founded by women's clubs. Barnard continued to be a promoter for the library, informing townspeople where it was located, and noting that school district patrons from outside the city limits were also welcome.

One of the largest gifts of books to the library came in 1927 when Mrs. Homer Arnold gave 139 books to Barnard, mostly non-fiction.

As September 1927 rolled around bringing the start of another school year, the student newspaper once again applauded Barnard and his library, noting that he had spent the summer rearranging and cataloging old and new books. Since 1924, after accepting the job as librarian, Barnard had never taken a vacation. He worked continuously from that time until his death in 1948. Barnard apparently derived immense pleasure in feeling needed by so many people. And it should not be overlooked that he was also highly altruistic. He wanted to help anyone who wanted to learn from his books. In another respect, however, he anticipated the late-20th-century disease of "workaholism." He had carried to extremes the Puritan work ethic of his New England ancestors. He could no longer separate his life from his library and books; he had no life outside of it — hence, a classic workaholic!

The community of LaCrosse rewarded him for this intense dedication and hard work. They had no idea that what he was doing was perhaps not terribly healthful. However, if longevity is any measure of satisfaction and adjustment, then Barnard, who lived to be 85, was definitely not ruining his health. His work was his inspiration and incentive.

Another way of looking at his career is to view it from the standpoint that Barnard was on a permanent vacation. He was doing exactly what gave him the greatest pleasure and power in life. Thinking about resolutions for the new year, Barnard stated in a front-page newspaper article on January 5, 1928, that emphasis everywhere was increasingly being placed on getting an education. Yet education was not a process ending with school; it was a lifelong endeavor. School, according to Barnard, simply afforded ability, desire, and initial equipment. Self-education was what really counted, and the most desirable lifelong skill was knowing how to use a library.

But Barnard did not have much time to wax philosophical at the start of the 1927-1928 school year. The library benefit had to be planned for February 28th, and it was to be a vaudeville program in the high school. The Tuesday evening program was the biggest event in LaCrosse in early 1928. Every performance was a good one, it was reported, with many encores demanded by the audience. The Harmony Harmonicas, consisting of Clifford and Carlyle Thompson, Wilbur Weigand, and Ben Siebenlist, was an extremely popular group. The Tomboys jiggled and rattled their bones to banjo tunes. Marvelous Marcella (Wilson) gave humorous impersonations in full costume. Mrs. J. C. Meyers with her Singing Strings (mandolin) played two numbers, accompanied by Miss Little on the piano. Warbling Walt (Newman) sang two vocal solos with his wife's piano accompaniment. The Dutch Dancers, whose members included Anna Harvey, Rara Ryde, Helen Serpan, Mary Gillaspy, Violet Cheney, and Elizabeth Davison, gave a clever performance in costume including wooden tap shoes. All of these took second place to the highlight of the evening, the fashion revue. Mrs. C. P. Fyler and Kathleen Walker portrayed a grandmother and granddaughter as they narrated the revue from their generational perspectives. Twenty-three dresses, each from a different year, were displayed. The earliest was from 1855 and was worn by Miss Little. The grand finale had all models on stage as Mrs. L. V. Mellick sang "Songs My Mother Used to Sing," accompanied by Mrs. H. P. Forney.

From Barnard's viewpoint, the highlight of the evening was Mrs. H. J. Walker, president of the library board, announcing the newly created sustaining memberships for the library, rendering further benefits unnecessary. Each sustaining member was to give $1.00 per year. At the end of the vaudeville benefit, 56 people signed as original sustaining members. In addition to the memberships, the benefit netted $29.35 for the library. As a follow-up to the sustaining membership announcement, solicitors visited every home in the rural school district to sign up each family as a "booster for a very worth-while cause."

By the middle of March 1928, over 75 sustaining members had their names printed in the newspaper. The goal was to sign at least 100. The Farmers and Merchants State Bank of LaCrosse became the headquarters for the community-wide enterprise. In May, a new decision was reached, which would expand the number of people using the library. The library would be opened to all people living in Rush County, not just the rural high school district. However, those living outside the district would be required to become sustaining members by paying their dollar. By this time, there were already 125 members.

As summer came to LaCrosse in 1928, a new rule of the library was made public: grade school children should come to the library between four and five o'clock, the last hour of the work day, so that older patrons would not be disturbed throughout the day.

Amongst a flurry of snow and oil exploration, 1929 came to western Kansas. Rush County was in the midst of this activity. For Barnard, it was once again time to reflect on the accomplishments of his years as LaCrosse librarian. When he had accepted the job, the high school had 100 books, the city library was non-existent, and his personal collection consisted of 3,000 volumes. Five years later, Barnard had combined the three entities under one roof, and the collection totaled over 4,000 books and 8,000 magazines and journals. He had properly indexed every item. He took special pride in the reference tools available and in his own ability to help each patron who entered his premises.

Although the sustaining membership idea was an overwhelming success and benefits were no longer necessary, old habits die hard. February 1929 saw an official library event billed as "library entertainment," held to stimulate interest in the library. The entertainment turned out to be a concert by the high school music department. The high school orchestra performed first. They were followed by girls from a drama class in a play entitled *Spreading the News*, as well as by the boys glee club. The entertainment, and an excellent speech by W. H. Russell, a prominent lawyer, persuaded 60 new members to sign up for sustaining membership in the library.

The library association's calendar year began in October. At the October 1929 meeting, it was decided to allow the checking out of certain magazines for three-day periods. Those that could be checked out were *National Geographic, American, Good Housekeeping, Popular Mechanics*, and *Reader's Digest*. During that year, 138 new books were added, $174 was expended and $286 received. The library was in sound financial shape under the direction of a board that oversaw this aspect of Barnard's work.

In 1929, Barnard reported to the board that the city library owned 1,170 books and that during the year 1,126 books had been checked out. Barnard viewed the increased use of the library as being in harmony with the improvement of the entire community. Though Barnard was advancing in age, he continued to spend most of his time in his library. Citizens noticed that he was hard at work; nearly every night after 10 o'clock, the lights burned brightly in the library. Out-of-town newspaper reporters took notice of him and his accomplishments in librarianship. They continued to report that for its size, his LaCrosse library was the finest in the United States, or at least, the American West.

Visitors were always impressed with the fact that Barnard attempted and succeeded at meeting the needs of grade school children, high school teenagers, and LaCrosse businessmen, as well as the general public. One businessman stated that if he ever found a subject about which he knew little, Barnard could tell him in an instant exactly where to find the information, be it in a book, magazine, or journal. If it was one of the latter, he could usually tell the patron which year and sometimes which month the information had been published. It was apparent that Barnard was reading the material that the library received.

As the Roaring Twenties came to an end, Barnard and his adopted town of LaCrosse on the High Plains of Kansas were poised to grow and prosper in total harmony. In anticipation of the agricultural expansion in Kansas in the 1930s, Barnard had a phone installed at his boarding room in Mrs. Anna Showalter's residence. It was to be a kind of "farmer's hotline." Farmers and other more citified patrons of the library could call him the instant they thought of a question. He would write it down and go to work on it immediately the next morning. Barnard had a fondness for using new inventions to better serve his library patrons.

Sadly, for all of his creative services, loyalty, and dedication to the

The Barnard Library Association found that this "Womanless Wedding" event was one of their best ways to raise money for books during the desperate 1930s. (Photo, Elva Paustian)

Kansas men "in drag" for the cause of the library in LaCrosse. (Photo, Elva Paustian)

cause of education, Barnard remained the lowest paid staff member in the school district. At a time when the superintendent of the high school district received $280 per month and a classroom teacher received between $150 and $200, Barnard received $90. Perhaps those running the school system believed that they were granting Barnard a rare privilege by allowing him to work for them — an all too often recurring theme for dedicated educators.

Reinforced by previous successes, Barnard and the library board decided to hold another library entertainment in February 1932 in celebration of George Washington's 200th birthday anniversary. This bicentennial program, which included 75 people, was a community pageant celebrating Washington's life. As a result, 85 new sustaining members were added to the library association's rolls.

In the fall of 1932, Barnard undertook a project to survey the women of the community through their clubs in order to ascertain which magazines they wanted the library to carry. By this time, Barnard was subscribing to 100 periodicals. He believed that this number could be pared down and perhaps other more valuable magazines purchased. He encouraged patrons to bring him their old magazines from which he used clippings to make current-events packages for the students.

To further aid the students, Barnard purchased with his own salary two sets of encyclopedias: the 1933 *World Book* and the latest edition of *The Encyclopedia Britannica*. He also purchased and presented as a gift to the students of the high school a 50-volume set of *Chronicles of America*. He believed that students of history, especially those preparing to go to college, needed this resource. Barnard stated that this set was usually found at the better colleges and universities of the nation.

A back-to-school tradition anticipated by most of the high school students was Barnard's personal distribution of the library rules. However, this tradition was suspended in the fall of 1934 due to an infestation of white ants in the library. The entire library had to be moved from the southeast area of the high school basement to the study hall. This, of course, violated one of Barnard's beliefs about the separation of libraries from study halls, but the books had to be saved. Ever optimistic, Barnard announced that this move would make it more convenient for students to check out books since they would no longer have to leave the study hall to go to the library. Although many people, including students, helped

These hardy Kansas farmers supported Barnard's work to the degree of dressing in women's clothing for a fund raiser. (Photo, Elva Paustian)

with the move, Barnard insisted on doing a major part of the work himself.

Possibly because of the able student help, Barnard decided to begin a student aide program for the library in the fall of 1935. As he viewed it, an opportunity would be given to students to assist in the operation of the library. One or two students would be selected for each hour of the school day. An activity credit would be allowed for satisfactory work.

By the mid-1930s, Kansas was experiencing the worst drought on record and was rapidly becoming the Dust Bowl of the Great Plains. Because of the financial ruin of many farmers and the economic disaster in not only Kansas, but the entire nation, President Franklin D. Roosevelt developed a recovery plan of locally designed work projects. This, to Barnard and the people of LaCrosse, was at least one glimmer of sunshine through the haze of blowing dust. As a result of Works Progress Administration funding, a new library was built for the community. The city commission and the high school board of education cooperated in the venture. A site was agreed upon between the grade and

Barnard sporting his winter beard as he sits amidst his books in the LaCrosse High School library. (Photo, Elva Paustian)

high schools, and the building was to be constructed entirely of native post-rock limestone, 57x25 feet, with an office 25x13 feet, two rest-rooms, and a vestibule. The total cost of the project was $16,945. The federal government paid $10,991; the remainder was paid by the rural high school district of LaCrosse.

Limestone for the building was quarried beginning in August 1936. Ironically, the actual breaking of ground for the new building began during the week of Barnard's 73rd birthday, September 14, 1936. The building was completed on schedule in July 1937. Wasting no time, Barnard had all materials moved from the back of the high school auditorium to the new building by the third week of July. A new chapter in Howard Barnard's life was about to begin.

The new Barnard Library shortly after its dedication in 1938. The library continues to serve the LaCrosse community from this building. (Photo, Barnard Library, LaCrosse, KS)

Chapter 9

Yankee in the Sun

Wisdom is the Olive
That Springeth from the Heart
Bloometh on the Tongue and
Beareth Fruit in the Actions
— Howard Barnard, 1912

We the undersigned respectfully petition the Board of Education of Rush County Rural High School District Number One, to place the name, Barnard Library, upon the outside of the new library building, thus honoring Howard Barnard the librarian.

*W*ITH this solicitation, the members of the Barnard Library Association successfully influenced the naming of the new facility after their hero. The petition drive began in August 1937 shortly after the completion of the new limestone building and its immediate occupancy by Barnard. The members of the association reported that the sentiment throughout the county was nearly unanimous that the new building be called Barnard Library. They had visited every home, getting residents to sign the petition. For the few people not at home, they left petitions at Pokorny's Pharmacy and Harper's Drug Store in LaCrosse, to be signed later. It took two special board meetings to adopt a name, but finally the Rush County Rural High School District Board of Education officially recognized their new library as the Barnard Library.

On Thursday evening, July 28, 1938, 60 patrons and friends honored Barnard, meeting him at the new library and putting on a splendid program. It began with a review by Wilma Baker of Lewis Mumford's book *Culture of Cities*. The excellent review compared the growth of cities to the growth of families. Just as families grew and needed new housing, cities, too, grew and needed greater cooperation among citizens for mutual protection and cultural enjoyment. Barnard undoubtedly enjoyed this intellectual portion of the program. However, the evening soon became a testimonial to him. The president of the library board, Mrs. C. C. Cavin, began the accolades by thanking Barnard for the work he had done in completing the new library. She also reviewed his work in education in the city of LaCrosse. Following her, Mrs. F. G. Hall, another member of the library board, described Barnard's early educational career teaching in one-room country schools throughout Rush County. The county superintendent of education, Ed M. Nickel, heaped the highest praise on Barnard for his establishment of the Entre Nous School. If anyone there knew firsthand of Barnard's accomplishments, it was Superintendent Nickel, because he was one of Barnard's former pupils. At the conclusion of his speech, Nickel pointed out other former Barnard pupils, including Mrs. J. B. Williams, Emma Frye, and Mrs. B. H. Yawger. Each gave a short talk reminiscing about her association with Howard Barnard.

As might be expected, Barnard had the last word. After explaining the various departments of the library and the classification of books, he presented everyone with a picture of the interior of the new library. There, in the midst of his books, graciously recognized by the most important people in his life, Barnard must have beamed with pride as he

The Barnard Library Association's "Gay 90s" fundraiser on October 21, 1938. (Photo, Elva Paustian)

closed the library that night and walked home. He was certainly happy to be of service to the sons and daughters of his fellow pioneers, most of whom he had managed to outlive.

Many of Barnard's admirers observed a custom of his. Each night when he left the new library, Barnard would tip his hat in deep respect to the building and its books and say aloud, "Good night."

This library celebration was not the first, nor would it be the last, honor for Barnard. Two years earlier in 1936, the citizens of Rush County had chosen him as its most distinguished citizen. As a result, he was further honored by the state of Kansas. A Hall of Fame in Wichita was established in celebration of the state's 75th anniversary, and each county's honoree was inducted. One person representing the values of the state and of their particular county was selected. The names and pictures for each of the inductees were revealed in the fall of 1936. The residents of Douglas County, however, the home of the state's largest university, the University of Kansas, could not decide on only one honoree and thus persuaded the directors of the Diamond Jubilee celebration to allow them to induct four individuals, including the chancellor of the University of Kansas, Dr. Frank Strong.

Barnard was in good company. Among other famous Kansans honored was John J. Ingalls, singled out by John F. Kennedy in his *Profiles in Courage* as one of the most courageous senators who ever lived because of his vote against the impeachment proceedings of Andrew Johnson, 17th president of the U.S. Ingalls had also given Kansas its motto, *Ad Astra per Aspera*. Another inductee was Amelia Earhart, the pioneer aviator who was a native of Atchison. William Allen White, the Pulitzer Prize-winning journalist from Emporia, was also inducted, as well as Carrie Nation, the temperance advocate from Medicine Lodge; General Frederick Funston, American hero of the Philippine campaign of the Spanish-American War from Fort Riley; and artist John Stewart Curry, the choice of Jefferson County, whose most famous painting can be seen in the Kansas State Capitol, *Baptism in a Horse Trough*. At the time of his induction, Curry was the resident artist for the University of Wisconsin. Also honored was Charles Curtis, from Topeka, the only Native American to serve as vice president of the United States; and Walter Chrysler, the inventor of the automobile that bore his name, born in Wamego, Kansas. Barnard was impressed with each of these Kansans, but felt most fortunate to have been inducted with a fellow teacher, Thomas S. Huffaker of Morris County. Huffaker had been the first teacher of white children in the newly formed Kansas Territory in 1849. Prior to that time, Baptist and Methodist missionaries were teaching only Indian children.

While the "Dirty '30s" was an unpleasant decade for most Kansans because of the dust storms, it brought statewide fame and recognition to Howard Barnard. However, neither the fame nor the midday darkness from the storms daunted this industrious librarian. He kept an even composure and went about his book work. He especially enjoyed basking in the limelight when reporters from hundreds of miles away drove to western Kansas to interview him. In 1938, Fred Henney of the *Hutchinson News-Herald* made the journey to discover

> a bachelor with no children of his own who thought enough of
> the boys and girls of a western Kansas community that he

gave . . . every dollar he had to bring them better educational advantages.

Henney further observed that Barnard was

wrapped up in educational work . . . although now past seventy years old, giving his entire time to this work to which he has devoted his life.

In this same interview, Henney quotes Barnard as saying that his great-great-grandfather had come to America from England on the *Mayflower*. The facts do not bear this out, however. Perhaps Barnard was trying to make an analogy that Henney did not understand about his relatives coming to America and his own journey to Kansas, walking and riding in a covered wagon. He had referred to his voyage across America as *his Mayflower*. Or, perhaps Barnard was embellishing his own life story or simply trying to make it meaningful for the reporter who never heard of the ship *The Francis*, which had landed after the *Mayflower* in New England. Barnard's great-great-grandfather was, in fact, a passenger on *The Francis*.

Newspaper reporters, including Henney, mentioned Barnard's dress, particularly his felt boots. The fact that he conducted interviews inside the library in a whisper so as not to disturb patrons who were reading or studying impressed them. As a courtesy, they addressed him as Professor Barnard.

As the decade of the 1940s dawned, Barnard's physical demise began. Late in March 1941, Baker Hospital in LaCrosse admitted him because he could not shake a bout with the flu. For all of his book learning, Barnard was not terribly wise about nutrition, or at least he did not practice particularly good eating habits. It was another example of his work taking precedence. Then one Saturday evening, November 27, 1943, an automobile struck Barnard in downtown LaCrosse. In most small rural towns in western Kansas, Saturday night was the highlight of the week in the 1940s, excluding Sunday morning church services. It was the night that the farmers came to town. Barnard was taking in all of the excitement on the crowded streets when he apparently became confused and stepped in front of a car driven by Alburn Wolter. Barnard had been going from the Farmers and Merchants Bank to the LaCrosse State Bank, doing what we commonly refer to today as jaywalking. Citizens immediately recognized him and took him to Hadley Memorial Hospital in Hays. He had suffered a broken right leg, but was reported in satisfactory condition on Sunday morning and returned to his home in LaCrosse in time for Christmas 1943.

However, in the first week of September 1944, Barnard was back in the Hays hospital for further treatment of the injured leg. He summoned the nephew of his old friends, Al and Frank Start, one James R. Start. While the hospital stay was no fun for Barnard, it was enjoyable to visit with James and exchange stories about their respective roots.

The Start family was very similar to Barnard's. The Barnards had come to America from Durham, England, and the Starts had come from Devonshire. The Barnard family had arrived in New England nearly 200 years before the Starts, but Yankee blood ran thick through these two Kansans. Religiously, both families were strong Anglicans, but politically the Barnards were strong Whigs and later Republicans, while the Starts were strong Democrats. The Barnards had both Connecticut and New York ties, the Starts had only New York connections, having sailed into New York harbor in 1834 and locating on a farm in upstate New York near Utica.

Both families had distinguished themselves by helping to protect America with members enlisting in the Armed Forces. Barnard family members had served in both the Revolutionary and Civil wars; the late-coming Start family had one member who had survived the two bloodiest battles of the Civil War, Gettysburg and Fredricksburg. James Start's grandfather, Robert, had enlisted in the Union Army when he was 59 years old. His youngest son, James K. Start, had set out for Kansas about the same time as had Barnard. In fact, the Starts had arrived in Hays by rail in 1878 after first settling in Iowa, beating Howard Barnard to Rush County, Kansas, by six years. A friend from Larned had convinced the Starts to settle in Rush County rather than around the Hays area, pointing out that the Rush County land had timber on it.

By the time Barnard had come to live with the Starts, the elder James had turned his original frame home into a more spacious two-story stone house that was partially earth-bermed. The eldest son of James K. Start was Robert, who also took up farming in Rush County. He was named after his Civil War veteran grandfather and in turn named his son James R., after his own father. Alternating names in this manner was common in the Barnard family, as well.

While Howard Barnard had gone from sheepherder to cowpuncher to schoolteacher to librarian, James R. Start had gone from serious student to soldier to college student at Fort Hays Normal. At the time he visited Barnard at Hadley Hospital in 1944, James R. was a well-respected college professor of forensics and drama at Fort Hays State College, having obtained his Master of Arts Degree from Columbia University, where Frederich A. P. Barnard, Howard's uncle, had served earlier as president. Fort Hays State University later named its theatre located in Malloy Hall in Start's honor.

During the hospital visit at Hays, Barnard had asked Start to get a particular book for him. Start remembered going to the Hays Public Library, finding the book, and taking it to Barnard, thinking that the print was too small for an 80-year-old to read; Start could hardly read it himself. When he handed Barnard the book and asked if he could read the print, Barnard replied, "I surely can. I can read the smallest print." And this was without the aid of eyeglasses. Barnard had never needed glasses to help him read. Unfortunately, however, although his eyes were healthy, the rest of his body was having trouble keeping up. The broken leg had taken its toll.

Start remembered having a conversation with Barnard about the teaching of Latin. Barnard reminded Start that he had studied Latin in grade school in New York City in the 1870s. They both denounced the 1940s approach to foreign language, which left it for the high school curriculum. The men agreed that if languages had continued to be taught in the grade schools, America would have been multilingual by the 1940s. And that being the case, introductory foreign languages would not need to be offered in high schools or colleges.

Start and Barnard also talked about the Entre Nous School. Start had once visited the school because Barnard was a friend of the family and the school was located just five miles from his father's farm. Of course, most of the discussion centered around the school's library. Start remembered it as one of the finest he had known. In an article he later wrote, Start remembered Barnard for his enthusiasm for education and scholarship and said that he was certainly a man of the "old school" who believed in a liberal — even classical — education. Barnard's ability to interest young people in books and in learning how to study from them had especially impressed Start.

Following treatment in the Hays hospital, Barnard returned to La-Crosse in less than a week. By the middle of September 1944, he was back on the job as librarian. He returned to find that the library had run relatively well without him. Clara Van Osdol had done her usual good job of beautifully binding and repairing the books in need of such work. Evelyn Reed, who had been Barnard's only assistant since the construction of the new building, had continued his policies exactly as he had outlined them. Of particular interest was the ongoing record Barnard had insisted on keeping of each patron, child or adult, and of every book checked out of Barnard Library. His purpose was not so much to maintain internal library records as it was to provide a service to patrons, helping them make their selections.

In the fall of 1944, Barnard's fame spread to the main annual event in the state, the Kansas State Fair in Hutchinson, where a portrait of Howard Barnard entered in the competition by Larry's Photography of LaCrosse won first prize. The portrait captured Barnard's bald pate and the unruly hair on the sides of his head, his long white Santa Claus-like beard, his deep-set eyes, and his furrowed forehead. It was one of the few pictures taken of Barnard in which he showed his age.

Because of the interest generated by this photo and the earlier 1938 Henney article in *The Hutchinson News*, the paper sent a reporter to LaCrosse in December 1945 to bring its readers up-to-date on the life of Howard Barnard. From this article, several confusing ideas were added to the uncertainty of the Barnard legacy. The reporter stated that Barnard had only left New York after his father died; then later, he said that Barnard had been in Kansas several years when he received an inheritance upon his father's death. Neither statement was accurate.

The reporter left the reader with several other misconceptions as well. He stated that Barnard had never charged tuition at the Entre Nous School. In truth, he did, albeit a minimal one. Another erroneous statement was that the barn at Entre Nous had burned to the ground. Actually, teams of horses had helped tear down the barn prior to 1920 for the lumber after Barnard had lost the property to his debtors. The reporter got most things correct, however, and for the first time it was reported that

Howard Barnard in his eighties, with a well-worn boot. (Photo, Barnard Library, LaCrosse, KS)

locals and Barnard himself referred to the Entre Nous School as ENS. This fact was interesting, because according to the stationery Barnard had used, the official title was Entre Nous College, not School. The reporter also said that in December 1945 the flagpole at Entre Nous was still standing. This was undoubtedly correct.

Perhaps the best quote that the reporter was able to get from Barnard was his explanation of why he bid his library and its books good-bye each night. Barnard said,

> At my age one never knows what may happen before morning and I wouldn't want to leave without saying good-bye.

Possibly the best tribute to Barnard to that point in time was another article published that same month. Leota Motz, co-editor of the *Hays Republican*, wrote it for *The Kansas City Star*, and it appeared on December 30, 1945. While Motz included some of the same erroneous information as previous articles, she obviously had spent more time with Barnard than had other reporters, as she gave more details and related an accurate sequence of events in Barnard's life. Especially enlightening was her account of his being hired for his first cowpunching job because he had gained experience working with horses on the Erie Canal. This was probably true, although Barnard hated horses, and the animals he had worked with on the Canal were actually mules. The overall captivating theme in Motz's article was her story of a hardworking pioneer whose idealism finally paid off in the accomplishment of his lifelong dream — his library.

These articles contributed to Barnard's fame throughout Kansas and the Midwest. What remained on the horizon was for someone to come along and project his story nationwide. That task would fall to Ralph Wallace, whose story and pictures of Barnard appeared in the November 1946 issues of both *The Rotarian* and *Reader's Digest* magazines.

The Rotarian article began:

> If enduring achievement can be measured as riches, Howard R. Barnard, of LaCrosse, Kansas, is enormously wealthy. More than 60 years ago he was a penniless cowherd on the wind-cursed Kansas plains. Today he is 83 years old and still penniless. But he ranks as one of the great educators in the history of America's rural schools.

Wallace went on to compare Barnard to the great inventor, Thomas Alva Edison. He stated that Barnard's educational innovations in rural

America made him a "pedagogical Edison." He cited Barnard's work in establishing scientific agriculture courses, physical education for all students, military drill 25 years before Reserve Officers Training Corps (ROTC), a rural school library, and the first consolidated school. Wallace, in a captioned picture of Barnard, the photograph that had earlier won the prize at the Kansas State Fair, referred to Barnard as being Whitmanesque in appearance. Wallace continued:

> Authorities have called Barnard's innovations among the most important in all rural education. Yet I feel that is a totally inadequate description of what he gave his pupils. What he gave was himself. Howard Barnard was a kindly, selfless fanatic who deliberately turned his back on wealth and comfort to teach unlettered cowboys and pioneer children. . . . Salary? It was a trust fund for the children he taught. None of the country schools where Barnard presided ever failed to get an organ, bought from his meager savings. Or a new addition to the building, hammered together with his own hands. Or the latest books . . . in neat cases and racks.

Wallace told readers of Barnard's early life growing up in New York City. He also mentioned some of Barnard's famous Eastern relatives and attributed his early fascination with Kansas to the Philadelphia Centennial Exposition that he had attended. Wallace did not emphasize Barnard's trek to Kansas, and he left out the Erie Canal experience altogether. The early Kansas experience was Wallace's focus.

> . . . Howard opened his first school.
>
> The school had the sky for a roof and tufts of buffalo-grass for seats and desks. At midday hard-bitten cowhands and wide-eyed pioneer children gathered around to learn reading and writing from the first educated man they had ever met. Howard was small — 5 feet 3 inches and 110 pounds — but he dominated his rough companions by his own passion to learn. Textbooks were the classics from Howard's knapsack. The students did their lessons on wrapping paper from a grocery store.

The usual stories about Barnard teaching in one-room rural schools were recorded, as well as Barnard's contributions to the county Normal Institutes for teachers. However, according to Wallace, Barnard would not tell him why he wore felt boots. Wallace had to go to the town's physician to get the story. As one might suspect, Wallace wrote mostly about the rise and fall of the Entre Nous School. He even included a picture of the two-story, white-framed building that showed stone fence-posts lining the walk from the county road to the school's entrance. His greatest fascination with the school was with the physical plant. The kid-wagon barn, the auditorium that seated 300, the central heating system, and the miracle for that day and age — imported gasoline lamps — all impressed him.

> Barnard made Entre Nous a social and cultural center for the whole neighborhood. Preachers came every Sunday and Christian Endeavor met once a week. In the Summer there were ice-cream socials and musicals; in the Winter oyster suppers, Halloween and Thanksgiving parties, plays. "That was in the days before radios or cars to get you to town," one elderly farm wife told me, "and Entre Nous became the brightest spot in our lives. It taught us farm living could be *fun*."

The article concluded by mentioning Barnard's ongoing library work. He found Barnard to be energetic, bursting with new ideas, proud, and as competent a librarian as he had been a teacher.

> . . . Every Thursday afternoon, eager boys and girls up to 10 years of age crowd around a locked bookcase in which gleam 15 to 20 new books — fairy tales, *Huckleberry Finn*, a child's story of Daniel Boone. Every time a child takes out a library book during the week, a card with his name on it is dropped in a bowl. On Thursday there is a drawing and the lucky winner chooses his or her favorite volume from the bookcase of prizes. A sort of juvenile bank night — in a library! The books, as usual, are paid for out of Barnard's pocket. . . .

Certainly America owes Barnard a debt: for a profound lesson in selflessness, pioneer courage, and achievement.

The *Rush County News* in LaCrosse reported on October 17, 1946, that Barnard's life story would appear in *Reader's Digest*. The November issue was already on some newsstands by October 15.

Possibly as a result of the *Reader's Digest* article, a reporter for the *Topeka Daily Capital*, Joe DeGeorge, also wrote an article about Barnard that was published on January 26, 1947. DeGeorge reported that the townspeople often thought of Barnard as being "fussy." He quoted Barnard as saying in rebuttal, "Remember this, it takes a crank to get anything started."

As a result of the *Reader's Digest* article, hundreds of letters from all over the world poured in to the Barnard Library. A typical letter came from Lewis P. Orr, post-dated Tokyo, Japan, November 11, 1946. Orr's stateside home was Hendersonville, North Carolina. Orr said that he was writing for the thousands who felt as he did but who would not take the time to write to Barnard. He said,

> You can bet your shirt . . . it has been people such as you, unknown and unheralded, who have contributed most to the American way of life.

Many letters came in Christmas cards, since it was close to the holiday season. Others came from former students in the one-room schools Barnard had taught in, as well as some from LaCrosse High School. Educators across the nation wrote, and still more came from long-lost relatives or people who thought they might be related to his branch of the Barnard family.

One letter from a former pupil, Luella Schaumburg Hoover, was typical of those from his students. She began by saying that she was thrilled to see fame come to him, as she had been singing his praises for years. Her children had heard so many Barnard stories that they believed they knew him. Hoover went on to say that so many times she had thought about writing him to thank him for all he had done for her, but that she had never gotten around to it. The greatest tribute she paid to him was to say that he had gotten her interested in reading and that she had passed that along to each of her three children. They all were book lovers because of Barnard.

Another interesting letter came from Norman Howorth of Chula Vista, California, who believed that Barnard was a Christian because of his life "abounding in Christ-like deeds." He thanked Barnard for being a "devoted follower of the Master" and wrote that as a "humble disciple of Jesus, I salute you and will include you in my prayers."

Another former student, Helene Sandlin, wrote to complain that Ralph Wallace, in his national article, had left out the most important things Barnard had taught her and her husband. She considered them so important, in fact, that they were teaching all of their children and friends — how to open a new book properly and how to make paper-sack book jackets.

E. F. Adney of Carmel, California, recalled both fond and not-so-fond memories of living in western Kansas in the 1880s. He remembered the Great Blizzard of 1886, and how he had made ice cream by adding some milk and sugar. He was so moved by *The Rotarian* article that he sent two small tempera paintings. It was his wish that Barnard sell them to buy more books for the children of western Kansas.

Eileen Roth was moved to write from Pennsylvania. She would con-sider it a great honor to receive an autographed picture of Barnard, as she had previously received one from her other great hero from Kansas, General Dwight D. Eisenhower. She felt that communism could never ruin America as long as God had chosen Kansas and America as the birthplace of such great men as Ike and Howard Barnard. [She perhaps did not realize that Barnard had not been born in Kansas.] She concluded that if he was ever in Pittsburgh he should not let the hotel situation both-er him: "We are only 20 minutes from the city."

Ruth Walden, a librarian from Wheaton College in Illinois, wrote to thank Barnard for his contributions to the noble calling of librarianship. She viewed her job and his as noble because it was a "natural result of thinking and working for others."

From Grimes High School in Iowa, Colleen Lomax wrote Barnard on behalf of the entire freshman English class. They had read the *Reader's Digest* article as a project and believed it to be a good idea to follow up by writing. They had enjoyed "Great Teacher of the Plains" as a charac-ter story. She requested a personal letter and a snapshot for the school bulletin board. The Grimes students undoubtedly had identified with Entre Nous School, as Grimes High School had 37 pupils, 13 of which were in the freshman class.

Elura Phenix, from Leedey, Oklahoma, believed she was related to Barnard through a Texas-Barnard connection. Phenix recorded how her great-great-grandmother, who was Spanish, had married a Charley Barnard, whose brother, George Barnard, bought her from the Indians.

A letter from Washington, D.C., celebrated Barnard in a poem. Another came from Jesse Curtis, another former student, who lived in Cedar Rapids, Iowa. His daughter's college English teacher had asked if her father could come to the class and give a lecture on Barnard. He also mentioned that her art teacher was anxious for her to paint a portrait of Barnard, and he extended an invitation for Barnard to come to Iowa for that purpose. Because Barnard never answered any of his mail, Curtis must have persisted about the portrait, for Elaine Curtis arrived in LaCrosse in the summer of 1948 to paint him. Her portrait hangs today in the Barnard Library.

One of two typewritten letters came from Virginia Brumback of Los Angeles. She pleaded with Barnard to help her with her predicament. She had had a better-than-average early education, but she had not studied formally since. She had married an older man of prominence, a lawyer with a Stanford University degree and a leader in civic activities. Librarians in Los Angeles could not help her with a list of suggested books to read in order to develop a broader cultural background. She hoped that Barnard, being a compassionate librarian, could assist. She apologized for the time it might take him and suggested that he could delegate this task to an assistant if he wished. She especially was interested in music, art, and drama, which she said she knew nothing about. For the sake of her husband, she believed that some knowledge of economics and business would also be helpful. She said the cost of compiling a reading list was no object, and a self-addressed, air-mail (five-cent), stamped envelope was enclosed.

And finally a letter-writer from Hollywood, California, wanted to adapt Barnard's story for a motion picture and closed with ". . . I shall be very anxiously awaiting your reply."

The praise in the letters must have made Barnard proud, but he remained unimpressed, the same unspoiled, even-tempered Yankee.

On Sunday, September 14, 1947, Barnard celebrated his 84th birthday, and he continued to work at the library. However, in January 1948, he became seriously ill and was admitted to Baker Hospital in LaCrosse. In February, he was well enough to move to one of the Ryan Tourist Cabins in LaCrosse where he was cared for by Frank and Editha Ryan at their "automobile court." A good family friend, Clay Brewer, volunteered to stay with him.

The townspeople of LaCrosse decided that a gala benefit was appropriate. It would show their appreciation of Barnard as well as help raise funds to pay for his hospital and living expenses, since he had saved no money from the salary he had earned. He had continued to spend every cent on books for the library and the children of the community.

High school students and some of the faculty of LaCrosse High School presented the program on Friday, February 27, in the grade school auditorium: music, dramatic readings, and speeches. Norma Kaiser played a Grieg sonata on the piano. Leon Kearney and George Keith gave a brief introduction. Then Leon Kearney read two poems, "Southward White Herons" and "A Writer Sells His Wares." Mrs. Karl Grossarth sang a solo, and Kearney gave a book review. George Keith led a high school quartet in a number called "Character Sketches." Another solo, "Only a Memory," was sung by Everett Renberger. The president of the Barnard Library Association made a few remarks, and the program concluded with a speech, "Success, Our Destiny," presented by Leon Kearney. Donations were accepted for the Barnard Fund. As they had done so many times in the past, Mrs. J. E. Attwood, Mrs. F. G. Hall, and Miss Alma Grass helped with the fundraiser.

In the newspaper article summarizing the Barnard benefit, the editor referred to Barnard as a nationally known educator regarded as a prophet by fellow educators for his school consolidation ideas. The editor also said that Barnard thought more of books than he did of himself and told of his walking all night to buy a book in a neighboring town.

Although Barnard was seriously ill at the time of the benefit, his spirits were certainly lifted by the program. During that winter, Barnard missed many days of work at his library. However, by March 18, 1948, the newspaper reported that he was much improved and was able to resume "being downtown."

It was about this same time, according to his assistant, Rosa Sehnert,

Money was raised by the Barnard Library Association for Barnard's funeral, as well as his headstone. The city of LaCrosse donated a plot for burial in the cemetery. Howard Barnard died nearly penniless. (Photo, Allan Miller)

that Barnard had his "bad day." Everything seemed to go wrong for him. He became totally confused about the procedures for checking out books, and when she asked if she might assist him, he replied, "Yes, it's time you took over. From here on, you will have to take it alone. I just can't do it anymore." He pushed the ink pad, daters, and pencils across the desk to Sehnert, sat down in his chair, and never checked out another book. With that pronouncement, he had given up his job as librarian. After that, he occasionally walked to the library to visit briefly.

On December 9, 1948, Barnard was unable to eat breakfast, so Frank Ryan called a doctor, and Barnard was taken to the hospital immediately. He passed away a short time later at 10:40 a.m. The cause of his death was bronchial pneumonia.

Funeral services were held at 2:00 p.m., Monday, December 13, 1948, at the city auditorium, the only assembly hall in town that could accommodate the large number of people who wanted to pay tribute to their friend. A group of the city's leading citizens had met as soon as they had

One of the last photos of Barnard was this one done for Elaine Curtis, the daughter of his student Jesse P. Curtis, who painted his portrait. (Photo, Barnard Library, LaCrosse, KS)

Barnard's portrait, when he was 85, by Elaine Curtis, the daughter of Jesse P. Curtis, one of Barnard's former students who had moved to Iowa and was dumbfounded when he read about his former teacher in *The Reader's Digest*. The portrait graces the Barnard Library in LaCrosse, Kansas. (Photo, Allan Miller)

been notified of Barnard's death to plan the service and select a place of burial.

On the day of the funeral, nearly everyone in the community gathered to pay their final respects to Howard Barnard. Schools were dismissed, and students occupied the mourners' section near the front of the auditorium. The funeral was typical for the times; the casket remained open throughout the formal service. Rosa Sehnert stated that she and others could not help but view "the little gray-bearded man" during the service and reflect on his noble ideals and unselfish manner. The motto he had kept on his desk kept coming back to her:

> No person was ever honored for what he received. Honor has been the reward for what he gave.

Barnard at last belonged to the ages. He was buried in the LaCrosse City Cemetery on a plot donated by the city. The Barnard Library Association purchased a large marble headstone to mark the gravesite.

Unlikely American Hero

He is Not Dead, This Friend — Not Dead
But in the Path We Mortals Head
Gone Some Few Tufling Steps Ahead.
— Zippa Hall (Barnard Bronze Plaque Dedication, 1955)

SEVEN years after his death, Barnard remained a force in the western Kansas town of LaCrosse. He had made an impact on the intellectual, cultural, and educational lives of his fellow citizens. The townspeople gathered at the city park to dedicate a large bronze plaque in remembrance of an eccentric gentleman who had neither looked nor acted the part of a hero.

Even before his death at age 85, the myths about Barnard had begun. Death, however, had enhanced them. Who was this man? What did he stand for? Why had he become so influential? What made him so intriguing? The answers to those questions might explain why Howard Barnard had become an unlikely American hero.

One trait best remembered about Barnard was his absolute hatred of pretense and formality. In fact, it could have been these that caused him to leave his home in the East for the less pretentious and less formal lifestyle of the Kansas prairie. Even though he realized the need for certain ceremony and ritual, as evidenced by his opening services at his Entre Nous School, he seemed to shun most organized celebrations. Barnard stated many times that he found Kansas people to be more generous and kind than Easterners. He found many other qualities in Kansans lacking in the Easterners as well. Consequently, he believed that the Eastern U.S. was in a state of oppressive decline.

His informality and lack of interest in ritual helped explain why he was not a churchgoer. Kansas was a place where church attendance was expected. One rumor proclaimed that he was an atheist. He was not, but that became one of the myths. Had he been an atheist, he would not have opened each new school day with the reading of Bible verses, hymns, and prayer. And it is doubtful that he would have allowed various churches such as the Brethren and the Methodist to use his Entre Nous School for summer Bible school, as well as for other religious functions.

Although his religious background was Episcopalian, he never formally joined any church in Kansas. Still, he had close ties to many of them, and the townspeople accepted him, even if he seemed not to be much interested in the affairs of church. People concerned by his shunning of their churches should not have worried. Other than educational organizations, Barnard was simply a non-joiner.

Another personality trait remembered by many was his strong moral fiber. Barnard had a highly developed sense of right and wrong. This led to a strong belief in American democracy and in the rugged individualism that he found more prevalent in the American West than in the East. Interestingly enough, many of the Kansas individualists like Barnard had come from New England. His ideas of right and wrong even showed in how he instructed his library patrons to open a book and properly turn the pages. Nothing irritated him more than to have a library patron disrespect a book by turning the pages incorrectly or carelessly.

Barnard was an unlikely American hero! Still, his life took on heroic proportions because of his indomitable spirit. He represented the old-fashioned American ideal that it is the essence — the heart and soul — of the man or woman that counts and not the appearance. Today, Barnard might not make the six o'clock news in even the smallest of television markets unless it would be to hold him up as a curiosity.

If oddity is sometimes a characteristic of a hero, Barnard, especially late in life, would qualify. A librarian at the Barnard Library remembers that when she was a young girl working there, the women workers had to tell Barnard when it was time for him to change clothes, as he had a habit of wearing the same apparel until it was soiled and smelly. When it was suggested to him that he needed to change, he willingly obliged. He would walk several blocks to the local men's-wear store and buy the best shirt available, come back to the library, change the shirt, and hide the old one in the library stacks. When the workers came upon one, they would send it to the laundry, paying the bill out of their own pockets. When the shirts or, in some cases, trousers, were returned, they hung them in a back room. One of the workers would eventually suggest to Barnard that he wear one of them instead of buying a new one. They sometimes found paper wrappings full of Barnard's used underwear among the stacks of books, which they burned! These peculiar habits were not lifelong traits of Barnard's, but appeared only in his later years, when he was in his 70s and 80s. It all added to the mystique about his life.

Barnard's reported eating habits were also eccentric. Former students and teachers said that he often ate only one meal a day, if at all — usually at midnight. It was speculated that one reason for only one meal a day was to save money to buy additional books for his schools and libraries. Many old-timers said that Barnard literally would rather buy and read a book than eat. A display case in the Barnard Library foyer holds scratch pad notes that were handed to local restaurant waitresses. On these notes Barnard had written out his order in advance, apparently in order to lengthen the time he could spend in silence and undisturbed before eating his meal. It is quite possible that he was meditating or praying. Dudley Shutte of LaCrosse, who had worked for three years as Barnard's library assistant, however, remembered that when Barnard had roomed and boarded with his grandparents for about four years, he ate three meals a day and was cheerful and conversant at mealtime. Presumably, at various stages of his life, Barnard fasted, ate one meal a

In his 70s, Barnard wrote out his restaurant order on 3 x 5 inch lined "Time Saver Cards" in advance. He claimed it was to avoid wasting time and unnecessary conversation. (Photo, Barnard Library, LaCrosse, KS)

day, or ate heartily. But he never seemed averse to some good old-fashioned, down-home Kansas cooking.

Barnard was also a confirmed cat fancier. He frequently had at least one, and sometimes more, living in his library. When Barnard was high school librarian at LaCrosse, students often played tricks on him and his cats. In one instance, a student rolled dried red pepper in hamburger and fed it to the cat, causing it to run wildly throughout the library. Barnard did not have a clue as to the cause of the cat's strange behavior, nor did he ever seem to suspect a student of having done something to provoke it.

Perhaps Barnard kept his library cats to control rodents. In any case, Barnard's habit of caring for all living things meant that the library cats would come inside and reside in warmth; and he always provided milk and food. Unfortunately for the cats, many of the stories of student pranks involved picking up the cats by the tail and throwing them. This was, of course, done out of Barnard's sight.

Barnard's voice and speech mannerisms also set him apart from fellow Kansans. Although he had lost any hint of an Eastern accent, he always spoke in a raspy whisper. No one knows why, for on occasion he seemed quite capable of speaking loudly. Perhaps he had gotten into the habit from being in the library stacks for so long. He never let his stammer get in the way of his communicating about books to his patrons, and he was never embarrassed or apologetic for his speech.

The late American philosopher Joseph Campbell said that a hero is a man of self-achieved submission. Barnard fits that definition. He achieved harmony in his life, living every day with the greatness of mankind's accumulated wisdom found in his library books. In this sense he seemed to view himself as the gatekeeper of heaven. He certainly did not view himself as a god, but rather as a protector of truth and wisdom. Barnard's dream was that all who entered his library would find peace and harmony. That was what books were for, to give credence to these two laudable traits.

British historian Arnold Toynbee believed that the great heroes are men or women who have battled beyond local and personal historical limitations. For such persons, vision comes purely from the inner self. Consequently, the true hero is eternal and eternally reborn and, therefore, always new. Barnard battled past the naysayers when he erected Entre Nous College, and people recognized something good in his human spirit. Yet, perhaps the bigger battle for Barnard was when he lost his school and all the money he had inherited, and he had to deal with his perception of personal failure. Still, he did not give up and return to the East. He could not leave Kansas until he had repaid his debts and once again regained his status in the community as an honorable citizen. Then when he had managed some measure of success, he chose to remain in Kansas.

Heroes have exceptional gifts. Barnard was not especially bright in comparison to other members of his family, but his gifts, given to the first generation of Kansas settlers on the High Plains, were his love of learning and his love for books. Sometimes, but not always, heroes are recognized by their contemporaries. In Barnard's case, the women of the community recognized him first. They saw his innate goodness and his potential as a cultural resource.

Heroes usually achieve some triumph over some form of oppression, and Barnard was no exception. He did not overcome a foe in a physical way, for he was a man who could not even mount a horse. He obviously was not going to clean out a local saloon with his six-gun, especially since he never owned one. The oppression Howard Barnard conquered was of a moral and aesthetic nature. He overcame the wrath of a nega-

All that remains of Barnard's once extensive library are a few books preserved in a collection room in the LaCrosse library that bears his name. On the middle shelf is one of his many stereoscopes that he loved to teach children to use. (Photo, Allan Miller)

tive school superintendent and the doubts of many citizens who were complacent about the role of books and libraries in a frontier community.

In the final analysis, Barnard understood something espoused by theologian Martin Buber. He was able to cast off the bonds of his ego and find "Thou." Completely unselfish, he gave himself to his fellow Kansans and achieved happiness.

The Pawnee Indians of western Kansas who lived in close proximity to LaCrosse had an interesting ritual. During the ceremony of the Hako, celebrating the beginning of life, the Pawnee priest would draw a circle in the ground with his toe to represent an eagle's nest. This nest symbolized the dwelling place of safety for all God's children — the kinship group, the community, the tribe. Barnard's nest was western Kansas.

Selected
Annotated Bibliography

*A*LLEN, Oliver E. *New York, New York* (New York: Atheneum Press, 1990). This is, by far, the best history of New York City. The author is quite readable and documents his claims with notes and has included an excellent bibliography. The photos are also worthy of mention. He has excellent accounts of the draft riots and the building of the Brooklyn Bridge.

Barnard, Henry. *Pestalozzi and His Plan of Education* (Syracuse, NY: C. W. Bardeen, 1906). A revised and more thoughtful book on Pestalozzi than Henry Barnard's first book published in 1862.

Barnard, Henry. *Pestalozzi and Pestalozzianism* (New York: F. C. Brownell, 1862). The first major work published in the United States on Pestalozzi. In this book, Howard Barnard's great-uncle

Henry, established the concepts of Pestalozzi in the minds of America's early educators.

Burnham, Alan. *New York City: The Development of the Metropolis* (New York: Garland Publishing, Inc., 1988). This is an annotated bibliography of the late author's personal library of mainly architectural sources of the city: great drawings and photos of many New York buildings and bridges — the Brooklyn Bridge, the Statue of Liberty, etc.

Celebrating a Century: The 1876 Philadelphia Centennial Exhibition (New York: Phoenix/BFA Films, 1990). An award-winning, 30-minute film that recreates the nation's bicentennial celebration. It features a short segment on the Kansas/Colorado exhibit.

Cuban, Larry. *How Teachers Taught: Constancy and Change in American Classrooms 1890-1980* (New York: Longman, Inc., 1984). One of the books in the *Research on Teaching Monograph Series*. Especially helpful and interesting to this book is "Part I: Progressivism and Classroom Practice, 1890-1940."

Dale, Kitty. "Howard Barnard: Santa on the High Plains," *Hays* [Kansas] *Daily News* (Dec. 26, 1971). An updated story of Barnard based on previous newspaper accounts. Of special importance are the photodocuments of Entre Nous School. This article kept many of the Barnard myths alive.

Downs, Robert B. *Henry Barnard* (Boston: Twayne Publishers, 1977). This is another short biography of Henry Barnard that features an excellent chronology of Barnard's life and accomplishments. It also has an interesting chapter on Barnard's attachment to the cause of library development in the United States.

Fisher, Sherla Lee. "Development of Education in Rush County," Master's thesis, Wichita State University, 1935. This thesis puts Barnard within the context of education throughout western Kansas, particularly Rush County.

Forsythe, James L. *A History of Fort Hays State University* (Topeka, KS: Josten's American Yearbook Co., 1977). One of the better college and local histories, written by the Dean of the Graduate School, a historian in his own right. There are references to Josiah Main and the development of the Normal School with which Barnard was familiar. Also, there are good references to James Start, whom

Barnard considered one of his friends.

Franzwa, Gregory M. *Images of the Santa Fe Trail* (St. Louis, MO: Patrice Press, 1988). The author recently traveled the Santa Fe Trail route and has documented his travel with pictorial works and historical notes about the trail that Howard Barnard heard of and tried to follow, albeit after the trail was replaced with the Santa Fe Railroad.

Fuller, Wayne E. *The Old Country School: The Story of Rural Education in the Middle West* (Chicago: University of Chicago Press, 1982). The best-documented treatment of America's one-room country schools. The last chapter is an excellent discussion about school consolidation.

Fuller, Wayne E. *One-Room Schools of the Middle West* (Lawrence: University Press of Kansas, 1994). An updated "coffee table" book of Fuller's earlier, more scholarly one. The narrative and numerous photographs make this volume easy to read for both academicians and lay historians.

Furer, Howard B. *New York: A Chronological and Documentary History* (New York: Oceana Publications, Inc., 1974). This is an annotated chronology of the major events in the development of the city of New York from 1524 to 1970. Many significant documents are reproduced, as well as a useful bibliography of New York sources.

Grass, Jennifer J. "An Early Educator: Howard Barnard." This Foundations of Education class theme, done in 1972 at Fort Hays State University under the direction of Professor Gordon Price, was well organized and based on various Rush County sources.

Gutek, Gerald L. *A History of the Western Educational Experience* (Prospect Heights, IL: Waveland Press, 1987). The most readable textbook for courses such as History of Western Education. Gutek is a Pestolozzian scholar, and his sections on the master Swiss educator are deep and enlightening. Included are two excellent chapters: "Pestalozzi and Natural Education" and "The Diffusion of Pestalozzianism."

Gutek, Gerald L. *Pestalozzi and Education* (New York: Random House, 1968). The best scholarly work on Pestalozzi in modern times.

Hall, Zippa. *Rush County Kansas — A Century in Story and Pictures* (LaCrosse, KS: Print Press, Inc., 1976). Contains a major article on Howard Barnard and his work in education and libraries written by

Margaret Hair. It also gives insight into his affiliation with the Barnard Library. The author replaced Barnard as head librarian upon his retirement.

Harris, William T., ed. "Henry Barnard," *United States Annual Report of the Commissioner of Education for 1902* (Washington, D.C.: Department of the Interior), vol. 1. Harris edited a series of articles about different phases of Barnard's life. Especially useful was the chapter by A. D. Mayo, a minister who knew Barnard. Much insight is given to the beginning of the Office of the Commissioner of Education.

Hibbs, Benjamin. "Kansas Cowboy Who Built His Own College on the Plains," *The Kansas City Star* (June 6, 1926). Ben Hibbs was a journalism instructor at Fort Hays State University at the time he interviewed and wrote this colorful account of Howard Barnard. Hibbs later became editor of the *Saturday Evening Post*.

Higgins, Shirley, and Carolyn Thompson. *History of McCracken, Kansas, 1887-1987* (Hays, KS: Printcraft Printers, 1987). One of the better local histories of a small Kansas town. Excellent photographs. This was a good source documenting Barnard, his schools, including Entre Nous, and his affairs about town.

LaCrosse [Kansas] *Republican*, 1913-1938. This was the leading local newspaper in the community to which Barnard moved upon the failure of his Entre Nous College near McCracken. This was an important resource in following Barnard's life in the LaCrosse community.

Legleiter, David. *Howard Barnard's Books* (1982). This is the only known inventory and listing of the books in Howard Barnard's personal library at the time of his death. It was compiled in partial fulfillment of the requirements of a Master of Science degree at Fort Hays State University and given to the Barnard Library in LaCrosse, Kansas.

MacMullen, Edith Nye. *In the Cause of True Education: Henry Barnard and Nineteenth Century School Reform* (New Haven, CT: Yale University Press, 1991). For well over 50 years, Henry Barnard's life has been in need of reinterpretation, updating, and major revision. MacMullen heeded the call and has produced an excellent and authoritative work. It is the singular most accurate biography of

Barnard and also of any of the early American educators of the Common School Movement. It is well written and includes the important stages of Barnard's life. It also has a helpful chronological listing of Barnard's written works.

Marcuse, Maxwell F. *This Was New York!* (New York: LIM Press, 1965). A good, easy-to-read history of New York designed for the average reader. It is extensive and is accompanied by excellent photos showing the city's history. There is no documentation to the author's interpretation of the city's history.

McCracken [Kansas] *Republican Enterprise, 1887-1913.* It was quite by accident that in looking through some of these past issues on microfilm, it was discovered that Barnard wrote a weekly educational column for this newspaper over a period of ten years. It is also a credit to the Kansas State Historical Society, Topeka, that a decision was made many years ago to preserve all newspapers printed in the state of Kansas. Without that decision and the perseverance of the Research Division to carry out the mandate, this book would not have been possible.

Miller, Nyle H. *Kansas: The 34th Star* (Topeka: Kansas State Historical Society, 1976). A pictorial history of the state.

Motz, Leota. "Cowpunching Kansas Teacher Gave His Fortune to Education," *The Kansas City Star* (Dec. 30, 1945). Motz was one of the first women newspaper editors in the nation. She, along with her publishing husband, founded the *Hays* [Kansas] *Daily News.* She wrote this story for *The Star*, apparently at their request, after interviewing Barnard several days after Christmas in 1945. It is very inclusive, accurate, and well written.

Oliva, Leo E. *Soldiers on the Santa Fe Trail* (Norman: University of Oklahoma Press, 1967). One of the best works on the Santa Fe Trail as a military route. A standard in the history of the West.

Paustian, Elva. Interview by Allan Miller (Spring 1990). The present librarian at the Barnard Library and a colleague of Barnard's at the library.

Pestalozzi, Johann Heinrich. *Leonard and Gertrude*, Eva Channing, tr. (Boston, MA: D. C. Heath, 1907). Pestalozzi's own masterpiece on how children should be taught and treated.

"Pioneer Dream," *Denver* [Colorado] *Post* (Mar. 12, 1956). This article recalled the story of Barnard and especially how the citizens of LaCrosse, Kansas, kept his memory alive by the building of a library in his honor.

Rodecap, Vera Ellerman. *The Country Schoolteacher: A Kansas Legacy* (Holton, KS: Bell Graphics, 1993). Already into its third printing, this small book is a marvelous collection of one-room school memories from those who taught in and attended them. The excellent introduction by Daniel C. Fitzgerald perfectly sets the nostalgic, yet balanced, stage. Several of the more than 200 oral histories of one-room school teachers collected at Fort Hays State University as part of the Plymouth School Museum are highlighted.

Rush County [Kansas] *News.* By 1939, this newspaper had supplanted the *Republican* as the best newspaper in LaCrosse and Rush County. It gave accurate accounts of Barnard, his library, and his dealings until his death in 1948.

Sehnert, Rosa. Interview by Allan Miller (Spring 1990). One of two surviving colleagues of Barnard, who worked alongside him at the Barnard Library in LaCrosse.

"A Short Grass Light That Failed," *The Kansas City Star* (Aug. 10, 1913): 49-50. The first regional and national story that told of Barnard's noble experiment, Entre Nous College, on the High Plains or, as *The Star* editor suggested, in short grass country.

Shutte, Dudley. Interview by Allan Miller (Spring 1990). Worked as an assistant to Barnard at LaCrosse High School as a high school student.

Socolofsky, Homer E. *Historical Atlas of Kansas*, 2nd ed. (Norman: University of Oklahoma Press, 1988). The authoritative reference work for maps of Kansas, the Santa Fe Trail, and the various railroads crossing Kansas.

Steiner, Bernard C. *Life of Henry Barnard*. Department of the Interior Bulletin No. 8 (Washington, D.C.: Bureau of Education, 1919). This is an excellent 100-page biography of Henry Barnard. It includes an interesting reminiscence of Barnard by David Camp when Camp was 96 years old.

Stephenson, Beckie. "Impressions Made in the Midwest: A Biographical Sketch of Howard Barnard" (1985). A Master's degree project in the College of Education, Fort Hays State University, which, among other things, does an excellent job of identifying unpublished works about Barnard.

Strate, David. "Howard Barnard — Sodhouse Scholar," *Up from the Prairie* (Dodge City, KS: Cultural Heritage Center, 1974), 15-18. This is a short, but well-conceived biography of Barnard and his place in Kansas history.

Taylor, Virginia, and Darlienne Werhahn. Interview by Allan Miller (Spring 1990). Sisters who knew Barnard and who had relatives who attended schools in which he taught.

Thompson, Darlienne. "Entre Nous College," *The Aerend*, vol.10 (1939). The best article on Barnard. This article was written by Darlienne Thompson Werhahn while an undergraduate student at Fort Hays Kansas State College. It is based on interviews she conducted with Howard Barnard in November of 1937. It provided a wealth of information and a source of inspiration to this book.

Thompson, Ruby. Interview by Allan Miller and Carolyn Thompson (Spring 1990). The only surviving student of Barnard's Entre Nous School.

Wallace, Ralph. "Great Teacher of the Plains," *The Rotarian* and *Reader's Digest* (Nov. 1946). This is perhaps the most glamorized article about Barnard; however, it certainly brought him well-deserved fame. After it appeared in *Reader's Digest*, Barnard received hundreds of letters from well-wishers. The town of LaCrosse, Kansas, was put on the national map.

Wyld, Lionel D. *Low Bridge! Folklore and the Erie Canal* (Syracuse, NY: Syracuse University Press, 1962). Looks at the famous canal from a literary as well as historical point of view with good illustrations and an excellent bibliography.

Zornow, William F. *Kansas: A History of the Jayhawk State* (Norman: University of Oklahoma Press, 1957). A standard college textbook for Kansas history courses. A necessary reference for Kansas subjects.

Appendix

Barnard Family History

*B*ARTHOLOMEW Barnard. Born between 1566-1570. Married Katherine Stanley, August 26, 1589, at Houghton le Spring, Durhamshire, England.

Bartholomew Barnard, II. Came to America from England on *The Francis*; he was descended from the Barnards of Barnard Castle, County Durham. Born 1591. Married Alice Weedon, August 13, 1626. Died May 13, 1663, in Boston.

Bartholomew Barnard, III. Born 1627 in Boston. Married Sarah Birchard on October 25, 1647, at Hartford, CT. Died 1698 in Hartford, CT.

Sargent John Barnard. Born 1650 in Hartford, CT. Had a child by Elizabeth Church of Hartford, CT. Died in 1734 in Hartford, CT.

John Barnard, II. Born March 1705 in Hartford, CT. Married Mary Case of Hartford, CT, in 1730 (second wife). Died February 11, 1771, in Hartford, CT.

Captain John Barnard, III (American Revolutionary War Hero). Born December 25, 1732, in Hartford, CT. Married Rebeckah Holcomb of Hartford, CT, on November 26, 1750. Died December 28, 1813, in Hartford, CT.

Chauncey Barnard. Born November 16, 1764, in Hartford, CT. Married Elizabeth Andrews of Hartford, CT, on February 4, 1802. Died March 5, 1837, in Hartford, CT. *Two of his children were Chauncey Barnard, II (Howard R. Barnard's grandfather) and Henry Barnard, First U.S. Commissioner of Education (Howard R. Barnard's great-uncle).*

Chauncey Barnard, II. Born in 1806 in Hartford, CT. Married Harriet T. Barnard of Charleston, SC, on April 20, 1838, at Hartford. Died December 25, 1876, in Goshen, NY.

Chauncey Barnard, III. Born January 26, 1841. Married Harriet W. Barnard of Hartford, CT, about 1861, a second cousin to her husband. Died February 4, 1925, in Middletown, NY. *Howard R. Barnard's mother and father.*

Howard R. Barnard. Born September 14, 1863, in New York City. Died December 9, 1948, in LaCrosse, KS.

Author's Note: The Barnard family is one of America's oldest, with many distinguished members. Frederich A. P. Barnard, president of the University of Mississippi in University, near Oxford, and Columbia University in New York City; Edward Barnard, discoverer of Barnard's Star and the fifth satellite of the planet Jupiter; and William Barnard, inventor of buttonhole scissors and armor plate for boats, first used in the American Civil War.

Index

by Lori L. Daniel

About the Artist

Michael Florian Jilg is a native Kansas painter and printmaker. He teaches the fall and spring semesters at Fort Hays State University and travels extensively in the summer.

A past Governor's Visual Artist, Michael has exhibited with or is a member of the Boston Printmakers; The Philadelphia Print Club; Santa Reparata Graphics Institute, Florence, Italy; Studio Camnitzer, Valdottavo, Italy, and has been awarded lifetime membership in the prestigious Gabinetto Desegni E Stampe Degli Uffizi in Florence.

His work has been published in "A Kansas Collection," "The Best of Kansas Arts and Crafts," "Erotic Art by Living Artists," and is represented in *Who's Who in American Art*.

Jilg's resume includes over 200 exhibitions and representations in museum collections in the United States, England, and Asia.